Wander Purposefully

By Eric Travis

Copyright © 2019 by Eric Frank Travis
All Rights Reserved.
Hardcover ISBN: 9781737136521
Paperback ISBN: 9781737136507
Audiobook ASIN: B07X634D6D
Ebook ASIN: B07WRF5P98

www.WeWanderPurposefully.com

First Edition.

Printed in the United States of America.

Written by Eric Travis.
Narrated by Eric Travis.
Published by Eric Travis.
Book layout and design by Eric Travis.

Special thanks to my early literary supporters, you know who you are.
Special thanks to Jenny(!!!), John(!!), and Max(!) for quality, low-cost (free) peer-editing.
Special thanks to Luke, Roger, Nicole, Dr. Doug, Megan, Beth, and Jay for support.
Special thanks to Marshall, Spencer, and Bob for inspiration.
Special thanks to Eddie for friendship.
Special thanks to my parents for giving me their best qualities and a fighting chance.

Dedicated to

JDRMJME

And

Jenny

Table of Contents

Preface	**8**
Introduction	**10**
Auditory Absorbent Learning	**30**
Visual Absorbent Learning	**68**
Experiential Absorbent Learning	**92**
Absorbent Learning as a Lifestyle	**138**
Conclusion	**190**
Epilogue	**202**
Trail Diary	**206**

Preface

Hello! There are a few things you should know before we commence.

Firstly, this is a nonfiction, self-help book. It certainly contains elements of other genres, including memoir, how-to, adventure, psychology, philosophy, and business. However, *Wander Purposefully* is primarily self-help. I hope you will not bristle at the mention of self-help. Unfortunately, the title of the self-help genre contains the implication that whoever reads the book *needs* to be helped, and whoever wrote the book has all of life's answers. This is hopelessly incorrect. Ralph Waldo Emerson said it best: "No man can sincerely help another without helping himself."

Secondly, this book was originally released in September of 2019 as an audiobook *only*. This was due to the fact that it was inspired by audiobooks I listened to while hiking the Pacific Crest Trail. My own personal inability to efficiently read self-help books in physical form meant my limited budget was better allocated towards the medium I personally would have preferred to consume. I also wanted to combat a false stigma I've noticed about audiobooks. I understand how the absence of printed words on paper and a physical book in your hands may be interpreted as if you didn't actually "read" the book. After you finish *Wander Purposefully*, you will have a deeper appreciation of the power of audiobooks as a supplement or substitute for physical books. In fact, throughout this book you will notice I use the words book/audiobook and read/listen interchangeably. This is because I don't believe there's a big difference between the two. Using some of my techniques, you can digest more books, and thus learn much faster, than you ever have before.

    Lastly, this book was published, written, researched, designed, formatted, recorded, audio edited, and narrated by me. I had zero experience in any of these pursuits before this endeavor. It was all outside of my comfort zone. You hold in your hands a concrete example of how leaving your comfort zone (and reading self-help books) leads to immense personal and communal growth.

Introduction

I didn't feel the urge to be one with nature. My life wasn't in shambles. My ideal day revolves around comfortable beds, showers, toilets, and shelters. I don't even especially enjoy hiking. Yet, I chose to spend one hundred and fifty six days hiking the 2,650 mile route from Mexico to Canada known as the Pacific Crest Trail.

Wander Purposefully, however, is not about the PCT. If you want a chronicle of the excruciating minutiae of trail life, check out the trail diary appendix that makes up the last quarter of this book. Rather, *Wander Purposefully* is about a learning process I feel compelled to share with the world. This process led me to the PCT, and catalyzed an immense, personal transformation whilst I was completing it. Most of all, *Wander Purposefully* is a commentary on what the vast majority of people choose to do in the "white space" of their lives. They do nothing. And that is a tremendous waste.

So what do I mean by **white space**? White space is a period in your day when you are performing an activity that needs to be done, but doesn't require critical thinking.

Take showering for instance. You need to shower to have socially acceptable personal hygiene. Therefore, you step into the shower and go through the physical motions of scrubbing, lathering and soaking. But what is on your mind during this time? For 2-15ish minutes of your busy day, your mind is allowed to wander aimlessly. It's allowed to wander because it doesn't have a choice. You can't use the touchscreen on your smartphone because your touchscreen doesn't work when it's wet. Let's face it, if it did, you'd probably be on your phone in the shower, too.

When showering, your mind does what people were forced to do all day before electronics — what we do nowadays for only a fraction of the day. It wanders. It thinks about your day. It thinks about nonsense. It even thinks about nothing at all. I've spent the better part of my life manipulating certain white spaces in my day, and putting them to work.

There are benefits to using our white spaces for things like silent introspection, contemplation, prayer, or meditation.

White space time is oftentimes used to ponder the tough problems and questions in our lives. It is in these luminary moments where important life questions surface, are acknowledged, and are answered.

Nonetheless, I will be presenting you with learning methods that are designed to invade and utilize this white space to help you further yourself in ways that would be otherwise impossible. I want to emphasize I am not telling you to utilize *every* white space of your day with my learning methods, but to choose to utilize them in certain white spaces of your day depending on your own, personal lifestyle.

It can be argued that by engaging in these methods, you will be introducing noise and distractions into spaces better left untouched. In my experience, nothing could be further from the truth.

By definition, meditation and the like occur within your own realm of experience. Therefore, you are meditating only upon what you already know, instead of discovering what you don't know. You are looking at the world through tunnel vision.

Over years of concentrated effort, I have amassed staggering foundations of knowledge. Because of this acquired knowledge, my mind is cantilevered to consider life's questions through lenses that include the peripheral vision required to experience epiphanies, and fully understand the bigger picture.

My learning methods *allow* those epiphanies to happen. I am not saying silent introspection, meditation, prayer, and contemplation should be cast aside. They are necessary to our continued growth and happiness.

I'm saying the times I do engage in those activities have been *enhanced* by knowledge I have gained via the learning methods I will share with you.

You can't schedule epiphanies, but you can make them more likely to happen.

To further this point, I want you to think about paradigm shifts. A paradigm shift is a realization that alters how we see the world. Controversial American author David Foster Wallace explains paradigm shifts in the form of a joke:

> There are these two young fish swimming along, and they happen to meet an older fish swimming the other way who nods at them and says, "Morning boys, how's the water?" The two young fish swim on for a bit and eventually one of them looks over at the other and goes "What the hell is water?"

The younger fish have been living in their world without thinking of water, precisely because it is everywhere. It is everywhere, and thus imperceptible.

Paradigm shifts change your prior conceptions of the world. Thus, the things you were thinking about before a paradigm shift occurs become obsolete. You, like the younger fish in the joke above, now know that water exists. This newfound discovery colors everything you *thought* you knew previously.

When you incorporate learning into certain white spaces of your life, you encourage more knowledge-induced paradigm shifts. Using my techniques, you will begin noticing the unseen water in your life. The moments in which we allow our minds to wander aimlessly are now *enhanced*. The white space of your day takes on a distinct purpose: to learn. You are allowing your mind to wander purposefully.

So, why is learning important for the world? Modern media has thrown a microscope on a large sector of the American populace who are cringe-inducingly ignorant of basic information. Comedy hosts and news anchors sometimes shine a light on this sector during popular segments known as "man-on-the-street interviews." These segments feature a microphone-wielding man walking amongst the public asking basic knowledge questions. They stroll along Venice Beach, Jersey Shore, or other locales, and discover many passersby are "hilariously" uninformed. A shirtless young man pontificates on the location of North Korea, pointing instead to New Zealand. A group of giggling high schoolers draw a collective blank when asked to name the date America received its independence. A hodgepodge of ill-conceived responses ("uhhh… January?"), and choruses of "I don't know" ensue. Unfortunately, I believe this conspicuous lack of basic knowledge contributes to the worst of society's ills. Alongside many sheltered, happy-go-lucky sanctuaries, racism, sexism, insert-your-own-ism, and warmongering afflict the macro societal environment.

How can anyone empathize with or respect another worldview if they lack the basic knowledge and experience to grant themselves any context or perspective on the matter? In a world with more communication capabilities than ever before, it is paramount to be able to interact respectfully with those with whom we disagree. One need only browse a social media comment section to find a free-for-all uproar inundated with the loud, angry, and opinionated. The truth is, many of these people who are wanting for knowledge and respectful discourse will become, or already are, bosses, influencers, elected leaders, and, perhaps most importantly, parents.

Remember, in *The Matrix*, when Keanu Reeves downloads a bunch of martial arts into his brain, and immediately becomes an expert martial artist? ("I know Kung Fu.") The techniques put forth in this book aren't exactly like that, but they're the closest we can get.

To help you manipulate your own white space, you need to understand how I came to be lucky enough to do it myself.

I was born on May 6th, 1993, and hail from the city of Yorba Linda in Orange County, California. I grew up on a small farm on a hill with my parents and four older brothers. My brothers are *much* older than I am. My youngest older brother was 8 years old when I was born, and my oldest older brother was 19. In fact, given my dad's advanced age and the passing of both grandfathers prior to my birth, I joke that my dad (a Vietnam veteran) counts as my grandpa, and my four brothers are like my four dads. I was an accident: "whoops, I thought I was menopausal," while simultaneously being a disappointment. My parents (especially my mom) desperately wanted a girl this time. Sorry, Mom.

When I was a kid, my bedroom consisted of two bunk beds, a couple dressers, an old beat-up air hockey table, and a big boombox blasting early 90s CDs like Nirvana, Blink 182, and Sublime. Three of the beds were taken up by my surly teenaged brothers, while I was predictably relegated to one of the bottom bunks. I was an energetic sporty goofball, trying hard and futilely to keep up with my brothers. My chief interest was playing sports, my preferred school subject was recess, my favorite movie star was Chris Farley, and my TV show of choice was NFL football. Had I continued on that trajectory, I would have likely become a one-dimensional jock in high school. However, my parents took a few actions during those tender years of childhood that would alter me psychologically and create unique sets of proclivities and habits for the rest of my life.

There is one action my mother took that must have seemed inconsequential to her at the time, but I believe has had cascading precocious influence on me throughout my life. I firmly believe I hiked the PCT because of this action, and it is also why I wrote this book.

When I was eight years old, my mother pinned a periodic table of elements print-out to the underside of the top bunk above where I slept. She tacked it right where I couldn't avoid seeing it at least twice a day. Every day I would lay there looking at it, either waking up or falling asleep.

This was the first white-space-turned-learning-tool I can recall in my life. I was a kid, I had no idea what the periodic table was. My mom was an English teacher, I doubt *she* even understood it. Nevertheless, I couldn't help looking at that poster every single day for years. Eventually, without really knowing what it was, I had it memorized. I *absorbed* it. I still know it today. I wasn't a child prodigy with a photographic memory. I studied a poster repeatedly and the information was eventually memorized. Throughout this book, I will be attempting to convince you, through psychological research and my own experiences, to believe in the positive causal effects of this form, and other forms, of what I call **Absorbent Learning**.

Absorbent Learning, as opposed to **Active Learning**, is learning done within our life's white space. It is a form of multitasking. We all unwittingly engage in Absorbent Learning. For instance, every time you hear a song during your day, you internalize a little bit of it. The more you listen to it, the more lyrics you can recite, and the better you can hum the melody. If you hear a song enough, you'll eventually know all the words, and the melody, by heart. If you heard it every day, you'd never forget it.

For that matter, we all engage in active learning. We actively learn whenever we specifically take time out of the day to do nothing but learn. When we go to school, do homework, or watch a documentary, we are actively learning. You are actively learning right this second because you are reading *Wander Purposefully* as a physical book. Active learning is crucial to our development as people, both when we are children and when we are adults. This book will coach you on how to include Absorbent Learning as a *supplement* to active learning.

Why should we supplement active learning? Because we don't actively learn enough. The problematic reason why we don't actively learn as much as we should is two-fold:

1. There are prerequisites that must be satisfied before you can begin active learning. You need to have the time, motivation, and resources to learn. After the day's activities, our energy meter is drained. Our motivation is low. We don't have time to crack open a book (if we even have a book to begin with). It's very easy to turn off the brain, turn on the TV, and take a break to spend time with loved ones. After all, we deserve it.
2. If we aren't vigilant, the information we've spent time actively learning eventually wafts into the forgotten cobwebs of our mind. I was an engineer in college, but just four years after graduation, I couldn't do a calculus problem if my life depended on it. I can't do it because I haven't spent every morning for the last four years doing calculus problems. I actively studied and learned calculus, then forgot it when I didn't need it anymore. If the information is now forgotten, what was the purpose of learning it in the first place? Calculus is lost in the chasm of forgotten information along with Pixar's Bing Bong (from *Inside Out*) and my other unused knowledge of the past.

Active learning is only useful long-term if you brush up on it all the time. Active learning can be useful in the long-term if you use Absorbent Learning afterwards. Most people are not going to sit down and do a calculus problem every day to keep calculus fresh in their mind (ain't nobody got time for that!). However, if I had placed calculus reminders in my white spaces and briefly refreshed the concepts every single day, I'd still know calculus. I could ostensibly relearn calculus via active learning, but I have neither the time nor the motivation required to do so.

It is important to note Absorbent Learning uses many of the same learning techniques as active learning. It's main differentiation lies in *when* we use it. We will be going in depth about the practice and the science of what I believe are the three major types of Absorbent Learning: Auditory, Visual, and Experiential. They are very different from one another. Let's define them:

1. **Auditory Absorbent Learning**
   This form is probably the most common form of Absorbent Learning practiced among Americans, though nobody calls it that. It entails *listening* with the intent to learn during white spaces in your day. Auditory Absorbent Learning introduces ideas in your mind, and stimulates thought processes that wouldn't otherwise happen.

   Unfortunately, Auditory Absorbent Learning didn't factor much into my life until shortly before I hiked the PCT. As an avid childhood reader of fantasy literature, I was dismayed at my apparent inability as an adult to read nonfiction self-help literature: books I believed could improve my life if I only had the patience to finish them.

   From a friend's recommendation, I experienced the wonder of podcasts, and began listening to them during my daily commute. I quickly got hooked. My podcasting commute turned into an audiobook commute, and then became my biggest motivation for hiking the PCT. I realized that if I were hiking the PCT, I would have a white space for the entire day. The only thing I would be doing all day long, for months, is walk and listen to audiobooks. By the end of my journey, I had completed 71 audiobooks (53 of which were nonfiction). I wrote this book immediately afterwards. This is what I refer to as my "PCT PhD," a very prestigious honor bestowed upon me by none other than myself.

Whether this doctorate of philosophy is valid is certain to invite debate, but know that I don't particularly care either way. This book is my dissertation. Later (during Part 1), I will dive deeper into how I accomplished my PCT PhD, the psychology of the Auditory Absorbent Learning approach, and what specifically you should spend your time listening to.

2. **Visual Absorbent Learning**

    We've already been introduced to Visual Absorbent Learning: that's what I was doing when I was staring curiously up at the periodic table as a kid. Visual Absorbent Learning is intentionally placing sets of information in white spaces, and then repeatedly absorbing the information. Visual Absorbent Learning distinguishes itself from Auditory Absorbent Learning because you engage with it to *memorize* desired information. I'd say this is also the type of Absorbent Learning that is least practiced by the populace, although multitudes have been exposed to it via the walls of the classrooms in their youth. Oftentimes, walls in school classrooms are littered with various Absorbent Learning materials like the ABC's, maps, or even periodic tables. I'd argue it's ironic we typically only place Absorbent Learning materials in locations where they distract us when we are supposed to be actively learning. School walls do not count as white spaces.

3. **Experiential Absorbent Learning**

    This is when you leave your comfort zone, thrust yourself into new varied experiences, and then absorb the effects. This is the hardest type of Absorbent Learning because it resembles active learning. You need to have time, energy, and resources to absorb in an experiential way. Experiential Absorbent Learning gives you the ability, and desire, to understand alternative points of view. This is essential for respectfully participating in the world around you. Experiential Absorbent

Learning is basically quality control for Auditory and Visual Absorbent Learning. It provides you with the outlook necessary to apply your acquired knowledge in ways that are ethical and empathetic. Thus, although it may be the most difficult, it is also the most important of the Absorbent Learning types.

After the periodic table kickstarted my unintended initial foray into Absorbent Learning, it took me years to realize the benefits of Absorbent Learning, and even more years to intentionally engage in it. During those tender childhood years, my parents also introduced me to my first major participation in Experiential Absorbent Learning. They forced me to join a choir. Far outside my comfort zone, I had to sing solo in front of live audiences — an absolutely terrifying experience for a little kid. My first solo (the first verse of *O Holy Night*) was so bad, even my mom didn't tell me it went well. My next hundred solos were progressively better, and I learned to calm my nerves in front of a crowd. As you'll read later on, my ability to sing well has played an important part in my life.

Fast forward a few years. When deciding which college to go to, I applied to Ivy League schools. The Ivys didn't accept me. Why not? Probably because (besides my many academic achievements) my high school resume was dominated by my all-league football accolades. If I was "too small" to be a Division 1 high school offensive lineman, I was definitely too small to be a collegiate offensive lineman. Harvard mailed me a simple rejection note. The only Ivy school to give me an interview was Princeton. This interview was a 10 minute coffee date with a dude who told me point blank I wasn't getting in. As such, you'll notice a tinge of sarcasm when I present academic findings from Ivy League scholars in this book. However, I thank them for the chip on my shoulder and for their unwitting academic support of my hypotheses.

I ended up having the "disappointment" to accept a generous scholarship at my Ivy-less safety school, Gonzaga University (Go Zags!). I ended up absolutely loving Gonzaga (located in the quirky Eastern Washington city of Spokane), and it holds a special place in my heart. Due to my undergraduate engineering major and my membership on the Gonzaga rugby team, I make periodic references to physics, chemistry, and rugby throughout this book.

My sophomore year at Gonzaga is when I first started to grasp and reflect on the positive causal effects the periodic table had on me when I was a kid. Knowing it by heart gave me a leg up on studying (when I actually sat down and did it), while also giving me opportunities to impress people. Having the table memorized is impressive because it's hard to memorize.

I didn't necessarily seek out situations guaranteed to showcase my elemental knowledge, but I did feel an affinity to go places where elements would be more likely to pop up. After starring at local trivia nights and such, I began to recognize the positive relational effects Visual Absorbent Learning was having on my life. I was the guy who knew all the elements, and that made me unique.

I first started to intentionally engage in Visual Absorbent Learning my junior year of college. I put up posters of the world map and a list of the U.S. Presidents in my shower. Over a couple years worth of 10 minute showers, I memorized the world's countries and their capitals, and could recite all of the presidents in order. I became the geography guy, the history guy, *and* the element guy. Pretty soon, I was stereotyped as the *smart* guy.

Trivial facts, like knowing the capital of Zimbabwe (Harare!) or the 15th President of the United States (Buchanan!), became anything but trivial. I had cultivated a personal brand of intelligence. Absorbent Learning made me seem smarter than I was before. And smart people get jobs. Smart people find significant others more easily. I'd say "smart" is one of the most frequent descriptors used when people are asked to describe their ideal romantic partner.

When you are in a situation where knowing the countries of the world is useful (more often than you would think, trust me), people who know them are objectively more interesting than people who do not. Smart people are *attractive* in a relationship sense, in a friendship sense, and as potential employees.

Smart and interesting are adjectives that never have a bad association when it comes to describing people. "I don't wanna be friends with that guy, he's too interesting"… said no one ever.

As a demonstration of the positive causal effects of Absorbent Learning, I'll share the story of how I met my wonderful girlfriend. We're going to get married one day. Jenny, a law student at Gonzaga Law School, decided she would go to the Star Bar on a chilly Thursday night in early December 2014. Star Bar was the shady, low-ceilinged, karaoke dive bar near campus that also doubled as a Chinese restaurant during the day. Gonzaga students only dared go here on Thursdays because of the special three-dollar "Long Island iced teas." Every other night of the week, the Star was reputed to be populated with sketchy drifters, so Gonzaga students stayed away. Jenny had never been there before. When she first walked in, I was on-stage singing the karaoke staple "I Want it That Way" by the Backstreet Boys. She heard me singing and approached me afterwards. She complimented me on my singing, we talked about our interests, and I found out that she studied abroad in Rome and had done extensive travelling. The rest, as they say, is history.

Some might call this a lucky chance encounter. That the "Stars" aligned. That we were both at the right bar at the right time, and she just happened to be attracted enough to me to come up and talk to me.

Let's take a closer look, however, to see how Absorbent Learning played a part in this defining event in my life. At this point, I had not yet undertaken Auditory Absorbent Learning, so this event was influenced only by my Experiential and Visual Absorbent Learning. Notice how many things I (an undergrad) had to do to even have a chance with her (a law student):

1. I needed to be a good singer. Good thing I had years of experiential voice lessons when I was a kid.
2. I needed to be confident on stage. Good thing I had loads of experi-

ence singing in front of an audience.
3. I needed to be (at least a little) physically attractive. Good thing I kept active by experientially playing rugby.
4. I needed to be smart, at least superficially. Good thing I was experiencing an engineering education at a university.
5. I needed to have similar interests with her. Good thing she liked travelling and, from my Visual learning, I knew every country and capital on Earth.

The fifth and last reason is what I want you to focus on. Not everyone is blessed with the opportunities and gifts needed to engage in certain types of Experiential Absorbent Learning: to be in a world class choir, or be outgoing on a stage, or play sports, or go to a private university. But most *everyone* blessed with a functioning brain and functioning eyes has the ability to put a world map in a white space and use Visual Absorbent Learning to memorize the countries on Earth. It's independent of privilege. It's independent of genetics. It's independent of how busy you are.

You can't download knowledge and insert it into your brain like Keanu Reeves in *The Matrix*. Your acquired knowledge is dependent only on consistent, intentional, daily effort. Knowledge doesn't move. Knowledge is just waiting for you to learn it. I firmly believe the little daily knowledge I had accrued through Visual Absorbent Learning maximized the serendipity of me and Jenny's meet-cute that December night.

The acquisition of knowledge is not only impressive, but it is also *achievable*.

The average person doesn't possess Freddie Mercury's immaculate larynx and subsequent four-octave vocal range; therefore, most people (me included) completely butcher the karaoke version of *Bohemian Rhapsody*. Most are not blessed with Shaquille O'Neal's 7'1" height; therefore most cannot dunk a basketball like he can. Drew Brees, current NFL record-holder for most career passing yards, is a shrimp by NFL quarterback standards (5'11"), but he has huge hands (the average male hand-span is 7.4 inches; Drew Brees' hand-span is 10.25 inches, the size you would expect from a man who is 7'3").

Lindsey Vonn, Olympic alpine skiing gold medalist, was blessed with parents who had the ability and finances to send her to an expensive and world-renowned alpine development program at 2 years old. By the time she was 17, she had climbed the skiing ranks to become a member of the United States Olympic ski team.

These people are anomalies. They were gifted extraordinary talents and/or opportunities, and had the wherewithal and work ethic to take advantage of them. The average person does not receive these opportunities. The overwhelming majority of people are not born with extraordinary physical dimensions like Freddie Mercury, Shaq, and Drew Brees. They are not presented with the opportunity to ski all the time like Lindsey Vonn (skiing is one of the most expensive hobbies you can have, trust me). People are forced to make do with the circumstances they are born into. Paraphrasing the words of Saint Francis de Sales, people are forced to bloom where they are planted, or die trying.

You may think memorizing the periodic table or knowing every country's capital means I have a freaky good memory. Not true. I don't have an especially good memory. From my extensive history of contact sports, (eight years of tackle football and four years of rugby), I've accumulated three documented concussions. I'm certain there were more that went undocumented.

Just as Isaac Newton said: "My powers are ordinary, only my application brings me success." With Visual Absorbent Learning, I have spent years (in ten minute shower increments) training my mind to memorize things other people do not memorize, precisely because those things are hard to memorize. With Auditory Absorbent Learning, I accomplished *decades* of reading within *five months* on the PCT.

The years I have spent practicing Visual and Auditory Absorbent Learning are composed of white space. White space is essentially **bonus time**: time ordinary people, who are not blessed with extraordinary abilities and opportunities, are able to take advantage of to make themselves extraordinary.

If I'm special in any way, it's my ability to learn just as well auditorily as I can visually. Though I share techniques for both auditory and visual learners in this book, it is important to note: many people do not learn equally well in both of these arenas. If you self identify only as a visual or auditory learner, I encourage you to at least attempt all techniques introduced.

You also might be thinking there's no point in learning things you could easily just look up on Google. Keep in mind, however, that the action of typing a query into Google takes a few seconds to complete. You are simply not afforded this time in social situations. Absorbent Learning makes information impressive in the relevant timeframes. It is more impressive to others if you can think quickly on your feet.

A year after I graduated from Gonzaga, I doubled down on my Visual Absorbent Learning. I created a spreadsheet listing fifty ways to say "thank you" in different languages, laminated it, and put it in my shower next to the presidents and world map. Nowadays, when I meet someone with a foreign accent, I ask them where their accent comes from. Nine times out of ten, I know how to say thank you in their native language, and I try to integrate it into the conversation somewhere.

My linguistic knowledge has been the most useful relational tool yet. It comes in handy at least once a week. For example, I was riding in an Uber rideshare and noticed the driver spoke with an accent. I asked him: "What accent is that?" and he responded saying he is originally from Ethiopia. I know from my shower wall that Ethiopians speak Amharic, and immediately hit him with a quick "Ah-meh-sah-guh-nah-loh" also known as "Thank you" in the Amharic language. The driver was astonished that a white guy from Southern California cared enough about his culture to know how to speak a word in his language. I impressed him within 10 seconds of conversation.

Loads of people speak Spanish, French, Italian and the other prevalent languages, but barely anybody speaks Amharic outside of Ethiopia and Eritrea. Be unique, learn one Amharic word, and you've made a small worldly connection to every Ethiopian and Eritrean you meet. That's almost 25 million people that you now have a small connection with. Perhaps more importantly, you become a worldly person to every other person you happened to be with when you met the Ethiopian. Now learn how to say thank you in Greek, Hungarian, Korean, Portuguese, Ukrainian, Swahili, Icelandic, Farsi, Vietnamese, et cetera, and suddenly you are the possessor of a small relational advantage whenever you come across someone who isn't American. Similar to the adjectives "smart" and "interesting," the word "worldly" is never a bad word to describe someone.

I would bet my bottom dollar I got a five star rating from my Ethiopian Uber driver, and I probably even brightened his day. After hearing a word in his native tongue, he might have gone home and had a new outlook on the city he lived in — a place he had thought was foreign to him in the extreme.

You also might be having ethical qualms over whether it is OK to learn superficial tidbits of knowledge with the intended benefit of seeming superficially smart or worldly towards others. I will counter this thought with the fact that the alternative to knowing small simple facts is *not* knowing small simple facts. We use active learning every day to learn things that can serendipitously benefit ourselves. Is sitting down to study for your math test also ethically wrong because you might impress someone with the educational degree attained by passing your math test? Chances are you're motivated to pay for and take that math class not for the love of math, but for the prestige having passed the class affords you. If there is an ethical problem with Absorbent Learning, there is the same ethical problem with our society's view on active learning. Much more on this later in the book.

What does smart even mean anyways? When "smart" is looked up in the Dictionary we find the definition: "having or showing a quick-witted intelligence." This effectively supplies us with the synonym intelligent. "Intelligent" is defined as: "The ability to acquire and apply knowledge and skills." These definitions clearly jive with my point. I've stated Absorbent Learning has made me *seem* smarter, but I would also argue it has made me legitimately smarter as well, just as smart, or smarter, as active learning makes me. After all, I have a better knowledge retention rate with Absorbent Learning than I do with active learning.

Absorbent learning not only makes you smarter, it also makes it easier to connect with other people. To convince you of this, this book will focus on how Absorbent Learning functions within the formation of **weak ties** and **strong ties**.

A weak tie is a person in your life who is not among your closest circle of friends, but can still act as a networking contact. They could be a slight acquaintance, or someone you bump into every few months. Weak ties may be more beneficial in certain areas of your life than even your best friends (also known as your strong ties).

It is a fundamental of human nature to gravitate towards those similar to ourselves. If we know our conversation partner cares and understands us, we are much more comfortable while speaking with them. In other words, we have a feeling of reassuring **attunement** when interacting with someone who knows who we are, where we come from, and how our minds work.

Let's briefly revisit the three types of Absorbent Learning introduced earlier, and how they can help use attunement to more easily convert strangers into weak ties and weak ties into strong ties. These three subjects will be the first three Parts of this book, followed by a Part explaining the connection between the three types of Absorbent Learning.

Part 1: Auditory Absorbent Learning — This is what I was doing when I finished 71 audiobooks on the PCT. The main use of Auditory Absorbent Learning is to expand our thought processes, and provide substance to help bolster weak ties into strong ties.

Part 2: Visual Absorbent Learning — Think of my serendipitous meeting with Jenny at Star Bar. I was better attuned to her interests and thus more attractive to her. Visual Absorbent Learning helps you transform strangers (people you have no prior connection with) into weak ties more easily.

Part 3: Experiential Absorbent Learning — Not only does Experiential Absorbent Learning help turn strangers into weak ties easier (like Visual Absorbent Learning) but it also helps turn weak ties into strong ties (like Auditory Absorbent Learning). The core advantage of Experiential Absorbent Learning is how it supplies you with a moral compass to guide and place into practice what you've learned.

Part 4: Absorbent Learning as a lifestyle — The fourth and last part delves into how Visual, Auditory, and Experiential Absorbent Learning work together to benefit the world and the learner.

So how did I get to the Pacific Crest Trail? After spending a couple years working as a project engineer in the Seattle construction industry, I felt I had a halfway decent business idea with this Absorbent Learning stuff. I was all too aware of the snares presented by entrepreneurship, so I thought it wise to learn as much as I could before making that big jump. I decided I would actively learn about business by getting my MBA at Gonzaga. Concurrently, I decided I would also take my newfound podcasting habit to the next level and listen to business audiobooks.

With my conviction that listening to audiobooks while walking was an awesome idea, I started taking the PCT dream seriously. Three weeks after finishing the graduate degree, I flew down to Southern California, drove to the Mexican border, queued up a bunch of audiobooks, and started walking north, to Canada. During my journey, I realized my business idea would make a better book than a business. *Wander Purposefully* became that book. You will read about my hike sporadically throughout the rest of the book, but you may also choose to read my trail diary contained in the Appendix at the end of this book.

Spoiler — I walked around 2,300 miles of the 2,650 mile PCT, starting in Mexico and finishing in Canada. To see Jenny and attend the many weddings we were invited to that summer, I skipped about 350 official trail miles in order to rendezvous several times with my best friend & hiking partner, Eddie. I also hiked many unofficial trail miles due to wildfires and various other circumstances. According to my Apple mileage tracker, I walked a total of 2,596 miles, or 99 marathons, over 156 days.

In the coming sections, I will often include research from an audiobook I listened to during my hike, and sometimes I will provide a footnote leading you to a picture of the scenery Eddie and I were walking beside while I was listening to that audiobook.[1]

The goal for this book is to make Absorbent Learning less of an esoteric idea. I am *not* saying you need to learn the details of every little thing on earth in your white space.

I'm saying it's *easy* to learn simple details if you apply my techniques, and you can glean immense relational benefits for yourself by doing so.

You will notice I stress the benefits of Absorbent Learning for the self. This is because I'm aware most people won't naturally (or always) prioritize actions

---

[1] To see a comparison picture of Eddie and me starting at the Southern PCT Terminus in Mexico and then posing triumphantly at the Northern PCT Terminus in Canada, you can use an internet browser to go to wewanderpurposefully.com, navigate to the picture menu in the Audiobook section, and click "Picture 1: PCT before and after"

benefiting their surrounding community, especially if there's nothing in it for them.

Absorbent Learning is *obviously* powerful for the self. The strongest reason why I felt compelled to write this book, however, is because Absorbent Learning can benefit the world we live in (take my Uber driver as just one small example).

This book explains how gaining perspective on other humans' ways of life, thus allowing you to foster relationships and more easily establish ties with them, can become a catalyst for global betterment.

PART 1

Auditory Absorbent Learning

Chapter 1

The Sims and You

"Three billiard balls can be pocketed with one shot."
— **ALEKSANDR SOLZHENITSYN,** The Gulag Archipelago

Absorbent learning is using learning materials in a place you frequently need to be (a white space). To illustrate what I mean by this, let's visit a computer game from my youth.

The Sims is the best selling computer game series of all time. It is a life simulation game where you control your own customized virtual human (known as a Sim), and lead him or her through a simulated American suburban life, complete with relationships, careers, and utility bills.

The game experience is largely dominated by your Sim's physical "Needs."

The Needs are as follows: Hunger, Comfort, Bladder, Energy, Fun, Social, Hygiene, and Environment. These needs are represented by 8 Meters in the lower right hand of your screen, and are visible whenever you are controlling your Sim.

Think of these Meters like a car's gas gauge. When your gas tank is full, the car runs, slowly draining gas while in use. When your tank is empty, your gas gauge is on E, and the car stops running until you fill it back up. Likewise, the Need Meter levels fluctuate as your Sim experiences life, just as they would in a real person's life. If your Sim's Bladder Meter hits empty (because you didn't command them to relieve themselves in time), your Sim wets his or her pants. Likewise, if you deprive your Sim of bedtime, their Energy Meter goes to zero and they fall asleep wherever they're standing.

Another foundational element of the game are your Sim's "Skills." There have been many sequels for *The Sims*, but in the first renditions there were just six skills: Cooking, Mechanical, Charisma, Body, Logic, and Creativity. Levelling up these Skills proves beneficial not only in the home life of the Sim, but is also the main determinant in whether or not your Sim is promoted in their chosen career path.

If your Sim has high Cooking Skill, they stop burning down their kitchen, start cooking meals faster, and start using recipes that satisfy their Hunger Need better. In their career, if your Sim is on the athletic career track, he/she cannot be promoted from a level 1 team mascot to a level 2 minor leaguer without progressing to level 1 in the Body Skill first. By the time you are at the top of the athletic track (a Level 10 Hall of Famer) your Sim needs to have a whopping 10 in Body Skill.

The way to increase your Sim's Skills is through practice. While they are practicing to increase their Skills, a blue Skill Meter pops above their head and is linearly filled based solely on how much time your Sim spends working on that Skill. If you want your Sim to increase their Body Skill level, you direct them to lift weights or swim in a pool for a while. But there's a catch. Going from level

1 in Body Skill to level 2 in Body Skill takes just a couple minutes, but continuing onto higher levels grows exponentially harder. The more Body Skill that's acquired, the longer your Sim needs to practice to go up to the next level.

Being the savvy game player you are, you may think you can simply command your Sim to lift weights, leave your computer to do something else, and return to your computer with your Sim's Body Skill meter full. Wrong!

There's another catch. You can't make your Sim lift weights and swim all day. Just like real life, your Sim has Need Meters. He gets tired, hungry, unhygienic, and uncomfortable after working out for a while. Your Sim's workout sessions need to be strategically scheduled with your Sim's Need Meters in mind in order to increase his Body Skill. In other words, your Sim needs to *feel* like working out to go work out. Sound familiar? Due to your Sim's Need Meter constraints, it would take hours and hours of gameplay to progress through Sim days, upgrade your Sim's Skills in their free time, and have your Sim be promoted in their virtual careers.

The popularity of the Sims franchise is directly tied to how much the game resembles real life. People, my former child-self included, find it fun to play pretend life. The parallels between the way Sims learn skills and the way real people learn skills are uncanny.

In his book *Outliers*, world-renowned author Malcolm Gladwell states:

> Research suggests that once a musician has enough ability to get into a top music school, the thing that distinguishes one performer from another is how hard he or she works. That's it. And what's more, the people at the very top don't work just harder or even much harder than everyone else. They work much, much harder. The idea that excellence at performing a complex task requires a critical minimum level of practice surfaces again and again in studies of expertise. In fact, researchers have settled on what they believe is the magic number for true expertise: ten thousand hours.

While 10,000 hours of practice is hard to visualize (the average lifespan is around 650,000 hours), Gladwell's point is salient. If we critically look at the action of acquiring knowledge, we realize that its acquisition is directly related to time. To progress beyond a novice level in anything requires extraordinary amounts of time. Inherent natural talents can shorten a particular person's practice-to-expertise timeline, but we are still essentially trading our time for skills.

Now think about Absorbent Learning and how it applies to *The Sims*. When I practice Auditory Absorbent Learning in real life, I'm on my commute (filling up my transportation Need meter) and listening to a book (filling up my Knowledge Skill Meter). When I practice Visual Absorbent Learning in real life, I'm taking a shower (filling up my Hygiene Need Meter) and looking at a world map (filling up my Geography Skill Meter) at the same time. If you were playing *The Sims*, and you could increase a Skill Meter during your Sim's shower, would you do it? Of course you would. Just like in real life, acquiring Skills in the Sims takes time. Your Sim needs to take showers anyways, or he starts emitting green stink squiggles and reeking up the joint.

Absorbent Learning would mesh your Sim's Need Meters and your Sim's Skill Meters so you could accomplish increases in both types of Meters at the same time.

If you would use Absorbent Learning in *The Sims*, why wouldn't you do it in real life too — where skills actually matter?

Chapter 2

A Thanksgiving Catalyst

"The superior man is distressed by his want of ability."

— **CONFUCIUS**, The Analects of Confucius

Two of my brothers are exceptionally well-read. Politically, one leans conservative and one leans liberal. During the Thanksgiving celebration after my last year of college (before I started Auditory Absorbent Learning), I listened to them debating a political topic of importance. I'm generally a decently loud person when it comes to parties, but when listening to this heated debate, I had nothing substantial to contribute. I was barely even part of the conversation (more a fly on the wall), but I was embarrassed I had no input. After some reflection, I came upon the realization that there were only a few topics of which I could speak at length learnedly and intelligently: principally, American football and my day job.

This Thanksgiving dinner conversation prompted me to take an unbiased look at how I was choosing to spend my time. I came back disturbed. I encourage everyone to do the same. Reflect on how you spend your time. Why do you spend it that way? What could you be doing instead?

Upon examination, my day job took most of my waking hours, and my relationships with Jenny and other friends occupied the rest of my time. On Sundays, I would regularly spend 10 straight hours with friends watching NFL RedZone and Sunday Night Football, cheering for my fantasy football teams.

I was having plenty of fun quality time with my relationships while having a steady income at my job. That seemed to be the way I would spend the rest of my life. Indeed, that is the way most people spend their lives. There's nothing *explicitly* wrong with that. You are cultivating deep relationships constituting purpose in your life. It's a pretty comfortable zone.

Still, I had this *gnawing* feeling. A distressing feeling I wasn't living up to my potential.

I began to reflect on how Visual Absorbent Learning had helped me make quick weak ties out of strangers. However, its effects were limited once I progressed past the initial stages of those relationships. I had loads and loads of superficial conversation fodder, but was lacking substance. Thinking back to that brotherly Thanksgiving argument, I realized books could provide me with deeper knowledge and substantial talking points.

The personal brand of intelligence I had started with Visual Absorbent Learning could be further strengthened by reading books. In due course, I decided to mix up my life priorities in an effort to insert more reading into my life. I determined Jenny, my family, my job and a few other choice friendships were the only things truly essential. First, I stepped down from the commissioner-ship of my fantasy football leagues, and informed my league mates that I would be quitting. I also chose to neglect some of the less meaningful friendships I was clinging onto, ceasing to actively try and spend time on them. Suddenly, I had some free time. I got right down to business, and began intentionally sitting down to read meaningful nonfiction books: books that would help my career while supporting my burgeoning dreams of entrepreneurship.

But there was a glaring problem. I couldn't concentrate. Since I was a kid, I've always enjoyed reading books. However, it soon dawned on me I really only enjoyed reading *fantasy* books. *Redwall*, *Lord of the Rings*, *The Chronicles of Narnia*, *Jurassic Park*, the extended *Star Wars* universe. Like many others, I read the whole 7th *Harry Potter* book on the day it came out. I couldn't put it down. I read the *Game of Thrones* series before it was even a TV show.

Conversely, when I tried to read nonfiction as an adult, my eyelids would start to droop before I even finished a paragraph. I wouldn't comprehend what I read, and would find myself re-reading the same paragraph over and over again to understand it. I couldn't even finish whole chapters in one sitting. I was interested in the topics, but it would take me *forever* to finish a nonfiction book.

I managed to read only three nonfiction books in my first year of prioritizing nonfiction reading. One of those books was former FBI hostage negotiator Chris Voss' *Never Split the Difference*. Voss' book demonstrates useful negotiation techniques; having to negotiate with construction subcontractors daily at my job, it immediately benefitted my work performance. I even asked for a raise (and was granted one) using the techniques Voss lays out in his book. I was floored at how readily the books I was reading positively influenced my life. The ways in which I viewed life situations were no longer only rooted in *my* life experiences, but also through new lenses provided by these authors.

Additionally, I noticed my vocabulary had improved. Words I had rarely used in the past became readily available to insert into conversation. My conversations were noticeably more meaningful. I noticed I was able to form persuasive opinions on the spot. Conversations that had before been rife with small talk, now had more substance to them. Previous weak ties were becoming stronger.

I was enamored with my apparent progression as an employee and as a person. Consequently, I grew incredibly frustrated with my inability to focus on my desired texts, and I classified completing only three books in a year as a monumental failure.

Shortly after that first year of prioritizing reading, a friend introduced me to podcasts on a road trip. I quickly got hooked. I discovered I was easily able to keep my concentration if I was driving at the same time. This was my first concerted effort to practice Auditory Absorbent Learning. I tried listening in my free time as well, but, just like with physical books, I couldn't concentrate at all if I was just sitting and listening. For some reason, I needed to be doing something else at the same time to keep my concentration fixed.

Soon, I began to see that as a positive. I could be doing my chores and reading at the same time (filling up my Need Meters and Skill Meters, just like *The Sims*!). A boring commute that had previously been filled with radio advertisements and songs I'd heard a million times before was now filled with *learning*. My commutes went by much faster, and I even looked forward to them. I began wishing my commute was even longer. So, I started walking to work. I got in a mini-workout, and I learned new things while I was at it. "Wouldn't it be great if all I had to do all day was walk? I could learn so many new things!" It was at this point when I started to think about hiking the PCT.

During this time, an offhand comment from one of my brothers prompted me to give audiobooks a shot. He told me when he first started working in a mind-numbing document review job as a lawyer, he listened to every one of Shakespeare's plays, and Edward Gibbon's enormous *History of the Decline and Fall of the Roman Empire*. Those were works I'd heard of since childhood, and I was drawn toward the idea of reading them. Though I very much enjoyed podcasts, I started to prefer audiobooks. I realized I could finally listen to the nonfiction books I was struggling so hard to read as physical books.

Podcasts aren't bad, I just prefer audiobooks. In general, people take hours, days, or maybe weeks, to prepare their podcasts. Books are an entirely different organism, oftentimes requiring years to complete. The greater effort expended corresponds to greater amounts of introspection, editing, and ultimately, greater quality. Though podcasts can be insightful, spontaneous, and funny, oftentimes there are whole segments dedicated to sponsorships and meaningless chatter. Those parts are a waste of time.

Throughout this book, I will stress the motif of time, specifically, the lack thereof. Time is your greatest currency. You should be spending your time as purposefully and efficiently as possible.

One way to make sure your time is more purposeful is by spending it listening to the highest quality programming possible. Programming that is time-tested, and represents the highest efforts provided by the human spirit. Sure, there are price tags associated with audiobooks (while podcasts are free), but that's because audiobooks are intrinsically more valuable, and thus deserve to be paid for.

Looking back, I gently kick myself when I recall all of my life's "white space" opportunities I've wasted doing nothing, when I could have been practicing Auditory Absorbent Learning. The biggest reason I previously resisted audiobooks is because I carried an unfair stigma against them: because they weren't physically in my hands, they didn't count as real books.

To combat that stigma, let's take a critical look at the action of reading itself. When reading a physical book, you are taking the time to look at words printed on a piece of paper, and silently dictating them to yourself. For example, while looking at the sentence preceding this one, the parietal lobe of your brain recognized the shape of the characters used, and their subsequent organization into familiar words. You then relayed that information throughout the synaptic architecture of your brain's neocortex, searching for comprehension.

When listening to audiobooks, you personally aren't expending effort to look at pages. You also aren't saying the words silently to yourself. Rather, some enterprising stranger (sometimes a celebrity) with a pleasant voice is dictating to you. The stranger is doing half the work. We seek shortcuts in every other part of our lives, why wouldn't we take this one?

In his book *Authentic Happiness*, prominent psychologist Martin Seligman discusses his life's shortcuts over breakfast:

> I am eating a toasted egg bagel with butter and blueberry preserves as I write this sentence. I did not bake the bagel, or churn the butter, or pick the blueberries. My breakfast is all shortcuts, requiring no skill and almost no effort.

It is beyond silly to avoid taking audiobook shortcuts when doing so is so clearly beneficial to us.

Furthermore, the stranger narrator of your audiobook recites more efficiently than you would. It's their job to know how the words should be pronounced, intoned, and delivered. How often do you waste time re-reading a sentence because you lost focus, or because you butchered the sentence's intended meaning by mispronouncing words or misinterpreting punctuation? Even the word "read" itself is pronounced differently in different contexts. It takes a second or so for our brains to decipher whether "read" should be pronounced like "red" or "reed." I've used both pronunciations multiple times in this chapter alone. Thus, absent expert speed-reading skills, audiobooks simply require less of your precious time to finish than physical books.

Audiobooks are also more physically convenient. You don't need to carry around a bulky physical book with you if you want to read one. They're weightless! As any PCT hiker will tell you, the weight of your backpack is under heavy scrutiny at all times. I've witnessed hikers break their toothbrushes in half to save those extra couple ounces of weight. Instead of lugging that physical book around, you can just pull your audiobook up on your phone, anywhere, anytime. If you're like me, fire alarms start blaring in your mind whenever your phone is unaccounted for for multiple seconds. You have your phone on you 24/7. Why not listen and learn as much as you can?

Perhaps most importantly though, the pertinent ideas behind the text are still being conveyed to you when listening to audiobooks. While you might not be able to behold the incalculable mystique and poetic structure of the physical words, it is a hell of a lot better to have listened to the book in your "white space" time than to not have read the book at all.

Do not confuse diminished experience with non-experience. How many times have you glared in contempt at the unread stack of books on your nightstand?

Physical books, read via active learning, suffer from some of the same general drawbacks as active learning itself. Yes, you finished the book, experienced its texture in your hands, and witnessed the poetic beauty of its vocabulary. However, you do not revisit the book every day thereafter. You will eventually forget what the physical words looked like. They will waft into the cobwebs of your mind. The elements of a book that stick with you are the ideas and characters the words themselves described.

That is exactly what audiobooks provide.

In a busy, technologically advanced world (where paper is increasingly being eliminated from our lives), it is time to realize the petulant folly of our audiobook stigmas. Embrace audiobooks. You will read more than you ever have before. Remember, I'm talking about Absorbent Learning — learning done in the white spaces of your life. Unlike with an audiobook, you can't do a secondary activity while reading a physical book. I don't recommend reading a physical book while driving or walking.

Chapter 3

Pacific Crest Trail University

As I mentioned in the introduction, I like to think I've earned myself a PCT PhD. I chose all my own electives, and specialized in general studies with a concentration in entrepreneurial business. It took me five months instead of five years.

The only issue with my "PhD" is others rightfully don't recognize it as a PhD. I never got that piece of paper. I can't wave it around (like many do) to demand respect or readership. Nevertheless, I know how much I evolved, and how much I learned, from these books. By the end of this book, you will know, too.

My PCT PhD was achieved by extreme Auditory Absorbent Learning. The following is the list of 71 audiobooks I completed while hiking the PCT.

1. *A Short History of Nearly Everything* - Bill Bryson
2. *Start with Why* - Simon Sinek
3. *Blink* - Malcolm Gladwell
4. *Modern Romance* - Aziz Ansari
5. *A Sand County Almanac* - Aldo Leopold
6. *The Lean Startup* - Eric Ries
7. *Fear and Loathing in Las Vegas* - Hunter S. Thompson
8. *The Martian* - Andy Weir
9. *The Subtle Art of not Giving A F*ck* - Mark Manson
10. *A Walk in the Woods* - Bill Bryson
11. *The Road* - Cormac McCarthy
12. *The Holy Bible, New Testament* - Narrated by Johnny Cash
13. *To Sell is Human* - Daniel Pink
14. *How to Win Friends and Influence People* - Dale Carnegie
15. *Dracula* - Bram Stoker
16. *Jab, Jab, Jab, Right Hook* - Gary Vaynerchuk
17. *Cadillac Desert* - Marc Reisner
18. *The Metamorphosis* - Franz Kafka
19. *The Art of War* - Sun Tzu
20. *A Confederacy of Dunces* - John Kennedy Toole
21. *The Autobiography of Benjamin Franklin* - Benjamin Franklin
22. *The Tipping Point* - Malcolm Gladwell
23. *Made to Stick* - Dan and Chip Heath
24. *Moby Dick* - Herman Melville
25. *The Prince* - Niccolo Machiavelli
26. *Ready Player One* - Ernest Cline
27. *Leaders Eat Last* - Simon Sinek
28. *12 Rules for Life* - Jordan Peterson
29. *The Perfect Storm* - Sebastian Junger
30. *Heart of Darkness* - Joseph Conrad

31. *The Holy Bible, Old Testament*
32. *Switch* - Dan and Chip Heath
33. *How to Fly a Horse* - Kevin Ashton
34. *Don Quixote* - Miguel de Cervantes
35. *The Omnivore's Dilemma* - Michael Pollan
36. *Crushing It* - Gary Vaynerchuk
37. *Walden* - Henry David Thoreau
38. *The Hard Thing about Hard Things* - Ben Horowitz
39. *The Shack* - Wm. Paul Young
40. *The Holy Quran* - Muhammad
41. *The Rise of Theodore Roosevelt* - Edmund Morris
42. *How to Write Non-Fiction* - Joanna Penn
43. *How to Write a Book that Doesn't Suck* - Michael Rogan
44. *Gulliver's Travels* - Jonathan Swift
45. *Being Wrong* - Kathryn Schulz
46. *Norse Mythology* - Neil Gaiman
47. *The Happiness Project* - Gretchen Rubin
48. *Guns, Germs and Steel* - Jared Diamond
49. *The Divine Comedy* - Dante Alighieri
50. *Never Stop Learning* - Bradley Staats
51. *The Promise of a Pencil* - Adam Braun
52. *Outliers* - Malcolm Gladwell
53. *The Gulag Archipelago* - Aleksandr Solzhenitsyn
54. *The Book of Mormon* - Joseph Smith
55. *The Long Walk* - Stephen King
56. *A Whole New Mind* - Daniel Pink
57. *Predictably Irrational* - Dan Ariely
58. *David and Goliath* - Malcolm Gladwell
59. *War and Peace* - Leo Tolstoy
60. *The Analects of Confucius* - Confucius

61. *Essentialism* - Greg McKeown
62. *The Iliad* - Homer
63. *SPQR* - Mary Beard
64. *The Book of Joy* - Dalai Lama, Desmond Tutu
65. *The Legend of Sleepy Hollow* - Washington Irving
66. *The Black Swan* - Nassim Taleb
67. *The Odyssey* - Homer
68. *The Happiness Advantage* - Shawn Achor
69. *Astrophysics for People in a Hurry* - Neil DeGrasse Tyson
70. *William Shakespeare: Comedies, Histories and Tragedies* - Peter Saccio
71. *Ulysses* - James Joyce

Here are some statistics behind the books:

- Total books finished: **71**
- Total nonfiction books: **53**
- Total aggregate length of all finished books: **879 hours and 42 minutes (36.65 days)**
- Average individual book length: **12 hours and 23 minutes per book**
- Longest Book: ***War and Peace* by Leo Tolstoy (61 hours)**
- Shortest Book: ***The Art of War* by Sun Tzu (1 hour and 14 minutes)**

To give you some context, if you are primarily a reader of physical books, here are some titles you may have seen before in audiobook length:

- *Wander Purposefully*: **8 hours and 55 minutes**
- *Harry Potter and the Sorcerer's Stone*: **8 hours and 33 minutes**
- *Harry Potter and the Order of the Phoenix*: **27 hours and 2 minutes**
- *Lord of the Rings: The Return of the King*: **18 hours and 19 minutes**
- *The Adventures of Huckleberry Finn*: **10 hours and 10 minutes**

- *To Kill a Mockingbird*: **12 hours and 17 minutes**

Note: Depending on the specific narrator's talking speed, different audiobook productions of the same books can vary slightly in length.

If the average length of my seventy-one books was about 12 hours, and the thickness of a physical book of that length is about 2 inches, I could stack all of my books 142 inches (11 feet, 10 inches) high. That's Shaq plus Peter Dinklage (on tiptoes).

Now let's compare my nonfiction reading performance before and after the trail: **Three physical non-fiction books finished in one year versus fifty-three non-fiction audiobooks finished in five months.**

Taking those numbers into account, I achieved a **1,766% increase** in non-fiction books finished, with an associated **59% decrease** in the amount of time expended to finish those books. If we make three non-fiction books per year a benchmark, I finished the equivalent of **17.66 years** (almost two decades) of non-fiction reading within the time span of **5 months**.

Those familiar with the PCT are aware of "challenges" that pop up within the trail community, sometimes serving to enliven the trail experience. Some popular challenges are the 24 hour challenge (hike as many miles as possible within 24 hours), the Oregon challenge (hike the entire Oregon section of the PCT within 2 weeks), and the McDouble challenge (hike a whole 100ish miles of the trail eating nothing but McDonald's McDouble hamburgers).

I'd like to introduce the **PhD challenge**. To complete the challenge, hikers will need to listen to a minimum of 879 hours and 42 minutes of audiobooks throughout the entirety of the PCT. Hikers choose their own specialty and concentration.

Chapter 4

How I did it

There are a few tools and techniques that immensely aided my learning efforts on the PCT, and could benefit those who wish to practice Auditory Absorbent Learning in their daily white spaces. My goal is to save you time, and to help you learn as efficiently as possible.

To spare having to screw around with an annoying mess of wires every time I took a break, I invested in wraparound Bluetooth headphones for my hike. Six days into the trail, I exhaustedly threw my backpack to the ground, neglecting to notice that one of my earbuds was caught on my backpack strap while the other was stuck on a shirt strap. Disaster! The right headphone ripped out of the intermediary charging port and I, extremely annoyed, thought they had broken.

However, the single left headphone still worked, and it was still attached to the charging port (luckily also still functioning). For safety reasons, I only listened using one earbud anyways because I wanted to be able to hear adjacent hikers and any malcontented wildlife that could be stalking me. The still-intact left earbud now nestled in my left ear, while the charging port, with its user-controllable volume, rewind/fast-forward and pause/unpause buttons, conveniently hung down past my left collarbone, easily manipulatable while tucked into my backpack strap. Thus, by shedding the right headphone (a couple ounces of unnecessary weight) and making the controls more reachable, I accidentally invented a new type of thru-hiker preferred headphone.[1]

Battery life was also a complication during my hike. Since I was frequently without cell service, I would conserve battery by putting my phone on airplane mode while I was hiking. Still, there aren't convenient charging stations on the trail. Outlets can only be found in towns along the way. In addition to my phone needing to be charged daily in order to listen to my audiobooks, I also had to charge my Bluetooth headphone multiple times a day.

To alleviate this concern, I chose to carry a relatively heavy-weight 10,000 mAh external battery pack that came with dual USB ports. I would charge my headphone with my external battery during food breaks, and, at night, I would use it to charge both my headphone and my phone. This way I'd be fully charged by morning, ready for another day's listening. If I was diligent about keeping my phone on airplane mode, the external battery would give me 6-7 days of juice, which is also about the maximum amount of time I would be away from any electrical outlet. While in town, I would recharge my external battery and be ready for the next multiple-day excursion.

My audiobooks were stored on my phone using an Amazon-connected app called Audible. When I got into cell phone reception, I used my phone to buy my desired audiobooks online via Amazon, and, within seconds, books were ready for download in the Audible app on my phone in my hand. No bookstores, no cash. I'd start the download, go do my laundry, and all of my new audiobooks would be downloaded and ready to go. On Audible, your

---

1   To see a picture of my unintentional headphone invention, go to wewanderpurposefully.com, navigate to the picture menu in the Audiobook section, and click on "Picture 2: Headphone Invention"

books are stored in a virtual library. You can switch books anytime you'd like, earn achievement badges, and view your listening statistics.

One of the coolest parts of Audible is the "Bookmark" function. After listening to a passage I found especially poignant or useful, I would whip out my phone, press the Bookmark button, and type out a personal note to attach to that specific bookmark. Sometimes, I would spend hours at a time with my audiobook paused, thinking about a specific passage. Afterwards, I could select a bookmark I had previously placed, read my personal note, and listen to the passage that prompted that note.

These bookmarks are why *Wander Purposefully* exists. I listened to all those audiobooks on the PCT, then took a month afterwards to re-listen to the hundreds of passages I had bookmarked. I used my personal notes to jog my memory as to why I thought the passages were useful. 68% of the quotes in this book are lifted from audiobooks I read on-trail or afterwards.

Another unintended benefit that accompanied so much listening practice is I became a better listener over time.

I experienced a listening compound interest effect. Audible has a function where you can speed up or slow down the narrator's voice. The standard narration pace is set at a "1.0" speed, but you have the option of slowing down the narrator to 0.75 or 0.50 speed, or going up to 1.25, 1.50, or even 2.0 speed. Setting your narration to 0.5 speed is akin to hearing paint dry, while a 2.0 speed setting is like being verbally accosted by a professional auctioneer.

As the trail progressed, I gradually noticed the narration felt slower. I was comprehending at a faster rate than the narrator was speaking. So, I began to increase my listening speed to 1.25 and eventually to 1.50 while still maintaining comprehension. Just as a speed-reader of physical books gets better at speed-reading through practice, I got better at speed-listening over time.

Consequently, if I hiked and listened to books for 10 hours in a day, I would actually be listening to the equivalent of 15 hours of my books during that time.

That is a 50% increase in listening progress in the same time period. I could finish a whole 15 hour book (like Bram Stoker's *Dracula*) if I wanted to listen to only one book that day. Conceivably, I could also read a shorter book multiple times if I wanted to (maybe John Steinbeck's *Of Mice and Men* five times over). However, for reasons that I will delve into in the next chapter, I typically varied the types of books I listened to depending on the time of day.

I have nothing but good things to say about Audible when it comes to my actual listening experience. But, there was one drawback. After a final tally, I spent more than $1,000 on audiobooks (an average of about $14 per book) in the form of periodic book purchases throughout the trail. This amount turned out to be much of my surplus discretionary income. Given that I would purchase new books after finishing the old ones, the dollars ascended to that lofty parapet without my full awareness. Then again, $14 per book is not extremely expensive when taken individually (about the cost of a cheap paperback), and the exorbitant dollar amount was more a result of the extreme quantity of books I listened to. At the end of the day, a thousand bucks is a cheap PhD.

Chapter 5

Flower Power

While I was hiking and listening to audiobooks, I would regularly experience what is known in the psychology world as a state of "flow." This term was coined by Hungarian-American psychologist Mihaly Csikszentmihalyi in the mid 1900s, and is the equivalent of saying you are "in the zone" or "feeling the groove." In his book *Flow*, Csikszentmihalyi describes one's flow as "the state in which people are so involved in an activity that nothing else seems to matter." Flow is a state of total absorption in the task at hand. A violinist regularly achieves flow while playing their instrument. Coders and writers do so as well when coding and writing.

Daydreaming is a common example of flow. Deep in thought, time slips by while you are on physical autopilot. Oftentimes, while immersed in flow, the "flower" will forget about temporal bodily Need Meters such as fatigue, hunger, and thirst. As such, flow is pretty useful when you are hiking up mountains and through deserts, tired, hungry and thirsty. Obviously, I wasn't flowing for the entirety (or even a majority) of the trail (there's not a flow off/on switch), but I eventually got better and better at achieving that state. When I was flowing while hiking, I would be deep in thought, formulating many of the ideas and opinions I discuss in this book, while also *not* thinking about my screaming bodily aches and needs. It made me more productive, and it made my days less terrible.

I knew I had the ability to flow because it would sometimes happen naturally. While you're flowing, you do not have a conscious realization you're flowing. It was only afterwards, after being distracted or shocked by an external force (say, a rattlesnake or a ferocious toe-stubbing), when I noticed I had been flowing in the first place.

When attempting to replicate my flow, three variables were the main determinants of whether I would start flowing or not. In *Thinking, Fast and Slow*, Nobel-winning psychologist Daniel Kahneman describes my first variable (effort) rather well:

> Accelerating beyond my strolling speed completely change[s] the experience of walking, because the transition to a faster walk brings about a sharp deterioration in my ability to think coherently. As I speed up, my attention is drawn with increasing frequency to the experience of walking and to the deliberate maintenance of the faster pace. My ability to bring a train of thought to a conclusion is impaired accordingly. At the highest speed I can sustain on hills, about 14 minutes for a mile, I do not even try to think of anything else… self control and deliberate thought apparently draw on the same limited budget of effort.

Through trial and error, I eventually discovered if I was maintaining a relatively constant hiking effort, naturally going a little slower during inclines and a little faster on declines, I had a greater opportunity to get into flow. The PCT is a perfect trail for this type of listening. The hills are more gradual and switchbacky than other long distance trails such as the Appalachian Trail along the Eastern US Seaboard or the Te Araroa Trail in New Zealand, whose inclines tend to be steeper and more sudden.

After neutralizing the effort variable, I found the state of my flow was directly tied to two other variables: how tired I was, taken in conjunction with which book I was listening to.

Towards the beginning of the trail, I tried to listen to Malcolm Gladwell's *Blink* for the entirety of the day. It is a fascinating book concerning the role that unconscious thought plays in priming our behavior. I easily achieved flow while listening to the first chapters. However, after an hour of concentrated listening and strenuous hiking, I found myself zoning out mentally as I correspondingly wore out physically. The more tired I was, the more often I would miss key points the author was trying to make. I was simply too tired to concentrate on every word, and a psychology book like *Blink* requires focus for comprehension.

Disappointed, I realized I could only listen to what I really wanted to listen to for only 1-2 hours per day. I seemed to be at an impasse because the amount of hiking I needed to do, and thus how tired I would get, was not subject to variability. If I was carrying three days of food and there were fifty-one miles until the next resupply opportunity, I would need to average seventeen miles of hiking per day or else I would starve.

However, I began to notice my fatigue progression each day was the same as the day progressed. I was most alert in the morning, and steadily lost my ability to concentrate in a constant downward sloping fashion. In other words, my tiredness, as the miles piled on throughout the day, would be predictable. I soon realized the complexity of the book I was listening to was the only variable that could be altered to compensate for my daily progression of fatigue.

After about a month or so of tinkering with my formula, I eventually settled on four tiers of books that I would read at four different points of the day, subject to how tired I was.

The Four Tiers were as follows:

1. **Early-morning non-fiction business/self-help/psychology books**
   (a la Malcolm Gladwell's *Blink* or Dale Carnegie's *How to Win Friends and Influence People* or Eric Travis' *Wander Purposefully*):

   These books rely largely upon a geometrical proof-based structure. The author introduces a subject, sequentially provides various supporting ideas/arguments/anecdotes that support each other, and eventually it all coheres to shape the author's big idea.

   This type of book is extremely reliant on the listener's concentration. If the listener zones out for a minute, they could find themselves missing a key definition or example referred to the remainder of the book, thus repeatedly confusing the listener and lessening their experience. This is exactly the reason I include the chimed sections in the *Wander Purposefully* audiobook. These types of books are usually no nonsense, get-to-the-point, how-to books on how to change your life right now. They aren't 30 hours long, they don't dance around with characters and cryptic metaphors, and they don't make you guess as to how to apply their lessons to your life. They tell you outright what, why, when and how you should be living your life.

2. **Late-morning history/biography books**
   (a la Mary Beard's *SPQR* or Jared Diamond's *Guns, Germs and Steel* or Edmund Morris' *The Rise of Theodore Roosevelt*):

These books still command the reader's concentration, but, as history is linear, the listener can afford to accidentally stop paying attention for a minute and miss things. Chances are the supremely important events will be talked about for at least a few minutes, and you aren't tired enough yet to zone out for minutes at a time.

In other words, the listening is easier, especially if you happen to be objectively interested in the specific history being narrated. I was more interested in Jared Diamond's *Guns, Germs and Steel* than I was in Mary Beard's *SPQR*, so I found that I could listen to *Guns, Germs and Steel* even if I was tired.

3. **Afternoon novels**
   (a la Cervantes' *Don Quixote* or John Kennedy Toole's *A Confederacy of Dunces* or Andy Weir's *The Martian*):

These books revolve around central characters the listener eventually grows attached to, and are thus easier to listen to. After being exposed to hours of characterization, Sancho Panza, Ignatius Reilly, and Mark Watney become emblematic of imaginary friends. You relate with them, and find it easier to pay attention to their stories even if you are tiring out.

4. **Evening religious texts**
   (a la *The Bible* or *The Holy Quran* or *The Book of Mormon*):

These books form the foundation of many people's daily thoughts and actions. They are also books where you can zone out for minutes at a time and not miss the main ideas. No matter how Christian you are, your salvation doesn't depend much on the width and length (in cubits) of the Temple of Jerusalem.

Thus, these books are just about the only thing that you can listen to when you're totally exhausted. They might even provide sorely needed inspiration. I was enlivened while listening to Johnny Cash narrating Revelation ("*And Lo, a pale horse!*") while I was summiting Mount Baden-Powell during a particularly grueling day on trail. [2]

In short, there were days of hiking in which I would listen to Malcolm Gladwell in the morning, a history of Rome before lunch, a Tolstoy novel in the afternoon, and then finish my day with the religious wisdom of Confucius.

If you are among the many who already practice Auditory Absorbent Learning: are there parts of your day when you lack the concentration and motivation to listen to a challenging nonfiction book? If there are, you could be switching that book out for one requiring less concentration, thus heightening your ability and likelihood to flow.

Could you be choosing your content more wisely? I believe Auditory Absorbent Learning should follow the variable precepts of Experiential Absorbent Learning. You should exit your comfort zone, and choose books you would not normally be able to read efficiently as physical books. This is what I did when I chose to listen to nonfiction during the PCT. I would have loved to listen to only fantasy books, but instead forced myself to choose books I would have trouble reading at home.

Exposing yourself to different types of literature enhances your ability to make weak ties out of strangers. If you love *Harry Potter*, how many times have you bonded with other *Harry Potter* fans?

As another example, let's say you are not a whaler, nor do you have any

---

[2] To see a picture of me and Eddie doing handstands at the summit of Mount Baden-Powell, go to wewanderpurposefully.com, navigate to the picture menu in the Audiobook section, and click on "Picture 3: Mount Baden-Powell"

interest in whaling. You are even vaguely convinced whaling is a detestable practice in general. What would happen if you read *Moby Dick*? You'd learn a little bit about whaling, your aquatic experiences from then-on would take on more significance, and you would be supplied with talking points and relational tools if you ever meet a seaman. What's more, there is the possibility your future boss, or maybe your future mother-in-law, is an avid fan of whales. After reading it, you don't even necessarily change your views on whaling, you are just unambiguously more informed about it.

Just because you read a book on a subject, doesn't mean you are then required to change your opinions. You now have a different vantage point on the issue. Kevin Ashton, in *How To Fly a Horse*, a book I listened to while hiking near Mammoth through the Sierra Nevada Mountains, introduces a concept known as *Shoshin*: "*Shoshin* is a word from Zen Buddhism meaning 'beginner's mind.' It refers to having an attitude of openness, eagerness, and lack of preconceptions when studying a subject, even when studying at an advanced level, just as a beginner would." We should all look at the world through this lens: to discard preconceptions about a subject and learn with an open mind.

While hiking near Mount Shasta in Northern California, I listened to Edmund Morris' *The Rise of Theodore Roosevelt*.[3] Teddy quickly became one of my heroes. In the biography, his literary versatility is apparent:

> The President [Teddy] manages to get through at least one book a day even when he is busy. Owen Wister has lent him a book shortly before a full evening's entertainment at the White House, and been astonished to hear a complete review of it over breakfast. Somewhere between six one evening and eight-thirty next morning, beside his dressing and his dinner and his guests and his sleep, he had read a volume of three-hundred-and-odd pages, and missed nothing

---

3   To see a picture of Eddie and me taking a bath in the McCloud River near Mount Shasta, go to wewanderpurposefully.com, navigate to the picture menu in the Audiobook section, and click on "Picture 4: McCloud River"

of significance that it contained.

On evenings like this, when he has no official entertaining to do, Roosevelt will read two or three books entire. His appetite for titles is omnivorous and insatiable, ranging from the Histories of Thucydides to the Tales of Uncle Remus. Reading, as he has explained to Trevelyan, is for him the purest imaginative therapy. In the past year alone, Roosevelt has devoured all the novels of Trollope, the complete works of De Quincey, a Life of Saint Patrick, the prose works of Milton and Tacitus... Samuel Dill's *Roman Society from Nero to Marcus Aurelius*, the seafaring yarns of Jacobs, the poetry of Scott, Poe, and Longfellow, a German novel called *Jöhn Uhl*... and Foulke's *Life of Oliver P. Morton*, not to mention at least five hundred other volumes on subjects ranging from tropical flora to Italian naval history.

This variety of literary tastes transformed Theodore Roosevelt into a conversational Swiss Army knife. I dub Teddy the King of Weak Ties. He could talk about anything and everything. If he couldn't, he would grill his conversant with questions until he *could* talk about it.

If Teddy can find time in his day to read, you certainly can too.

Chapter 6

A Powerful Motivation

"Incentive spurs effort."

— AESOP, Aesop's Fables

The miles took their daily toll, and there were moments on the PCT that were physically, mentally and spiritually taxing. In these desultory moments, it was all too obvious I was exposing myself to this hardship voluntarily. It would have been much easier to quit the ridiculous journey and go back to my comfortable mattress and life. During these moments, the audiobooks I listened to were my most powerful incentive. Keeping my three book per year reading baseline in mind, the more books I finished, the more productive I would feel. The more I could justify my time spent away from a job, away from Jenny, away from everything. Every three books I listened to, I had essentially achieved a mental milestone equivalent to a whole year of reading. Depending on the books I was reading, I sometimes finished six books in a single week.

Steve Kamb's book *Level Up Your Life*, describes an exceedingly effective way to create achievable incentives. Inspired by his past addiction to gaming, he took the tenets of immersive video games involving levels and boss battles, and applied them to real life by creating a "level structure." He reasoned that completing an intermediary level in itself was cause for celebration. Thus, the long journey to accomplish his goals was rendered more enjoyable with proudly achieved milestones. He would then be more likely to continue his journey and reach the end. When describing his strategy for learning to play the fiddle, he made the following six-tiered level structure:

- LEVEL 1: Commit to one violin lesson per week, and practice 15 minutes per day for six months.
- LEVEL 2: Relearn how to read sheet music and complete "Celtic Fiddle Tunes" by Craig Duncan.
- LEVEL 3: Learn to play "Concerning Hobbits" from the *Fellowship of the Ring* on the violin.
- LEVEL 4: Sit and play the fiddle for 30 minutes with other musicians.
- LEVEL 5: Learn to play "Promontory" from *The Last of the Mohicans* on the violin.
- BOSS BATTLE: Sit and play the fiddle for 30 minutes in a pub in Ireland

Authors Chip and Dan Heath discuss Kamb's level structure in their book *The Power of Moments*, and apply it to the way we normally pursue common goals, such as learning Spanish:

- LEVEL 1: Try to squeeze in a Spanish study session.
- LEVEL 2: Try to squeeze in a Spanish study session.

- LEVEL 3: Try to squeeze in a Spanish study session.
- LEVEL 4: Try to squeeze in a Spanish study session.
- LEVEL 5: Try to squeeze in a Spanish study session.
- DESTINATION: Someday, eventually: "Know" Spanish

I listened to business self-help books through the recommendations of those I respected with business world experience. The other books on my reading list, however, were chosen based on my own preferences. I had plenty of time everyday to think about which books I wanted to read next. When applying the Steve Kamb levelling system to those books, it would look something like this:

- LEVEL 1: Finish *The Martian*, a movie you like.
- LEVEL 2: Finish *Moby Dick*, your father's favorite book.
- LEVEL 3: Finish *The Bible*, a book you feel guilty about not having read.
- LEVEL 4: Finish *War and Peace*, the book you have always thought to be the pinnacle of huge books.
- LEVEL 5: Finish *Ulysses*, a book widely considered to be one of the most advanced reading-level books of all time.
- BOSS BATTLE: Write your own book.

Add my audiobook incentives together with my hiking goals, and I had a decently effective antidote for the dark thoughts that would sometimes enter my mind: a phenomenon known on-trail as the "darkies." These are thoughts and feelings pervading our minds that try to convince us to give up on our goals and quit.

Do you have your own darkies?

Times when you are lost in your own feelings?

Do you have milestones to help you cope with them?

Have you completed any milestones or boss battles of your own?

Chapter 7

Making Your Opportunity

"When the student is ready, the teacher appears."

— A BUDDHIST SAYING

If you don't have white space time in your day to listen to books, make some. The incredibly successful story of William Paul Young, author of *The Shack*, began on his commute to work. In describing how he found the time to write his self-published book, Young said:

> At the time I would drive 25 minutes into Gresham, and then hop on the MAX, the metro transit train, for 40 minutes each way to downtown Portland where I was working for a web conferencing compa-

ny… I decided that the MAX part of my commute would allow me the time to begin working on a project.

The Shack has sold more than 20 million copies, and has recently been adapted into a successful theatrical film. It would not exist had William Paul Young not had white space in his day. Young would likely still be working for web conferencing companies had he not written his novel.

A train ride is a white space where you can afford to not only absorbently learn, but also actively learn (read and write physical books). Your hands and brain are completely free to wander. It is what is known as a "dumb commute." Other dumb commutes include plane travel (where you are not the pilot), bus travel (where you are not the driver), and ferry travel (where you are not the captain).

"Smart commutes," on the other hand, are commutes in which you are personally piloting a vehicle. You have the opportunity to absorbently learn, but are not afforded the opportunity to actively learn because your hands are busy. Ironically, dumb commutes (where you can actively *and* absorbently learn) make you smarter than smart commutes (where you can only absorbently learn). Thus, if you currently have a smart commute, research ways you could make your commute a dumb commute. Take the bus or train instead of driving. If dumb commutes are not an option, make sure to get the most out of your smart commute white space with the Auditory Absorbent Learning techniques I've just described.

As we End Part 1, here are some takeaway Action Items for Auditory Absorbent Learning:

- Perform an unbiased inspection on how you choose to spend your day.
- Reflect on your learning goals.
- Identify white spaces in your day.
- Use an app like Audible, or similar, to obtain audiobooks or podcasts.
- Pick audio content that will be of the most use to you as a person. See the Auditory Absorbent Learning section of wewanderpurposefully.com for suggestions.
- Listen, learn, and take notes. Taking notes provides a permanent resource for you to easily recollect and retain your Auditory Absorbent Learning.
- Follow @etrav_learning on social media and join the Absorbent Learning newsletter for continual inspiration.

PART 2

Visual Absorbent Learning

Chapter 8

The Stans and You: A Love Song

L et's try my next method of Absorbent Learning: Visual Absorbent Learning!

It is my pleasure and delight to introduce you to the Stans. Most people know about Afghanistan and Pakistan, but fewer know much about their unheralded neighbors to the North: Kazakhstan, Kyrgyzstan, Tajikistan, Uzbekistan and Turkmenistan.

We will be returning to the Stans picture a couple times throughout the book and I will be coaching you on how to best visually absorb the information as we go. Imagine yourself performing your showerly routine, and casually looking over to this map. Spend a few seconds looking at it, sound out the names of the countries as you read them (they are surprisingly phonetic — Kazakhstan, Kyrgyzstan, Tajikistan, Uzbekistan, and Turkmenistan). Briefly familiarize yourself with the shape and size of the countries. There's no written test on this later, no pressure, no stress at all. My goal is to show you, through this simple example, how easy it is to practice Visual Absorbent Learning.

In my experience, "trivial" stuff like the Stans pops up all the time, especially if one is paying attention and expecting it.

For example, one time I was talking with an elderly distant cousin of mine who had spent lengthy periods of time in the Navy and Air Force Reserve. I hadn't seen him in years. We got to talking about his service and he mentioned he had been stationed in Kyrgyzstan during one of his stints. A light bulb went off in my head. Bingo! Time to utilize my Visual Absorbent Learning! I said, "Oh cool! Were you stationed in Bishkek?"

His jaw dropped in disbelief. He asked me how on Earth I knew the capital of the very remote Kyrgyzstan, of all places. I brushed it off, and told him I was just a fan of geography. But the damage was done, he couldn't help but be impressed.

Much later, this same cousin, who lives near Portland, travelled hours out of his way to treat me to a much appreciated meal on the PCT when I was traversing Mount Hood on the Oregon corridor.

I can guarantee this small absorbent-learning-fueled interaction contributed to the carrying out of his generous action.

Chapter 9

Optimus Prime

As you may know, primer is a building product that is lathered onto a material before applying the first coat of paint. Priming before painting optimizes adhesion of the paint to its intended surface, lengthens the paint's durability, and provides an extra layer of protection for the material being painted.

In the psychological realm, the concept of priming acts the same way. It is the act of preparing your brain for activities in the future. In essence, we know it as a much more common word: practicing.

A musician looks at a piece of music and practices until they have committed the notes to muscle memory, and can play it flawlessly by heart. The same goes for athletes who put in hours upon hours of practice to perfect their sport. Kobe Bryant used to practice by counting his made shots, only stopping when he had made 400. As many coaches have preached, practice makes permanent.

Though athletes and musicians are easily understood examples, people engage in priming all day long. Through daily recitation of the Pledge of Allegiance, Americans are primed to be patriotic from youth. The Nicene Creed is a similar priming used by the Catholic Church.

There are also horrible historical examples of priming, ranging from the propaganda machines of erstwhile super-powers, to the omnipresent, faux-immaculate images of the "Supreme Leader" in North Korea.

Though there are many negative primings we encounter everyday, we can take it upon ourselves to introduce positive primings into our lives.

Take my Visual Absorbent Learning practices as an example. My day starts with a shower. In my shower, I am learning. After I shower, I step out of my house with learning on my mind.

The priming effect fosters beneficial effects on children as well as adults. Looking at the periodic table when I was a child primed me to think about science first thing in the morning and last thing before bed.

I once read an autobiography about a young boy growing up in rural 1870's Massachusetts. This boy details his mother's efforts to prime him as a child (though he does not label it as priming):

> The boy, she said, was to build beautiful buildings… she took ten full-page wood engravings of the old English Cathedrals from 'Old England', a pictorial periodical to which the father had subscribed, had them framed simply in flat oak and hung them upon the walls of the room that was to be her son's… Before he was born, she said she intended him to be an Architect.

The boy's name? Frank Lloyd Wright — also known as the man widely considered to be the G.O.A.T. of American architecture. Would Frank Lloyd Wright have become an architect if not for his mother's priming? Given all the other potential professions, probably not. This is impossible to know, of course, but we can safely conclude he was more familiar with buildings than he would have been otherwise. Perhaps this familiarity, whether he realized it or not, was among the deciding factors when Wright chose his career.

This conviction of mine is supported by the existence of the mere-exposure effect. This is a term authored by Polish social psychologist Robert Zajonc, as well as a subject I became familiar with when I listened to Gretchen Rubin's book *The Happiness Project* as I crossed the California/Oregon border on the PCT.[1]

The mere-exposure effect suggests a person is more inclined to "like" a subject if they have been repeatedly exposed to that subject.

This finding is frequently posited as the main driving force behind the billions of dollars companies allocate to advertising costs every year. Marketing experts know the more times you are exposed to a product, the more likely you will buy that product. This is why catchy jingles exist, and why the same commercials repeatedly occur during the same television program. The marketers want the same people, who are assumedly watching a television program from start to finish, to be exposed to their products multiple times in one sitting.

My thinking on the subject of priming has been greatly influenced by experiments performed by psychologist John Bargh. One of these experiments involved Bargh and his team gathering college students and giving them an exercise to complete. The exercise involved constructing four-word sentences from a given set of five words (such as "*finds he shoots basketball the*"). For a single group of students, the given words contained words associated with geriatric old age, such as *bald*, *gray*, *wrinkle*, *Florida*, and *forgetful*. After the exercise, the groups would then be asked to walk down a hallway to another test station. Unbeknownst to the test subjects, the hallway walk was timed, and was also the whole point of the experiment. Those who had been *primed* to

---

1   To see a picture of the California/Oregon border that took us 106 days to reach, go to wewanderpurposefully.com, navigate to the picture menu in the Audiobook section, and click on "Picture 5: California/Oregon Border"

subconsciously think about old age during their exercise were found to walk significantly slower down the hallway, as an elderly person would, than those who had *not* been primed with thoughts of old age.

Due to the propensity for the elderly to move to Florida upon retirement, the experiment's findings are now referred to as the Florida Effect.

I had first heard of Bargh's experiment during the PCT in Malcolm Gladwell's *Blink*. Gladwell introduces his readers to the experiment by actually testing them with the five-words test instead of explaining it at length, as I just did.

I listened to *Blink* during the first few days of the PCT, and took the five-words test mid-hike. During the test, without knowing about the Florida Effect, I noticed my ankles starting to physically ache. They were most definitely not aching before the test began. I mentally brushed the ache off as a minor annoyance. When Gladwell explained how the test was supposed to make me feel, my ankles stopped aching completely. I was shocked. The effect was personally jarring to me because my father has increasingly suffered from extreme arthritis in his ankles as he's aged. This malady has grimly affected his ability to walk long distances. Thus, I specifically have been primed to associate ankle pain as an indicator of arthritis and old age.

Though Bargh's five-words experiment has had replication issues in subsequent unbiased experiments, my personal anecdotal experience stands out as singular proof in itself.

In his psychology book, *Thinking, Fast and Slow*, Daniel Kahneman also references Bargh's experiment, but his book delves much more deeply into how our brains are wired to think. The titular modes of thinking within that text are **slow thinking** and **fast thinking**.

Slow thinking is practiced when you are deliberately working a problem out in your head. Take the multiplication problem 207x62 for instance. Most likely, your brain cannot automatically supply the answer to this problem (12,834) because it has not memorized the answer yet.

Fast thinking, on the other hand, involves the usage of **heuristics**: mental shortcuts people automatically take when solving problems and making judgments. Prejudice and stereotypes are common examples of heuristic judgments. Intuitively knowing the answer to the multiplication problem 2x2 (without doing the math in your head), or knowing Lima is the capital of Peru are examples of heuristic problem solving.

Fast thinking is what Visual Absorbent Learning is all about. It is about taking trivial things that are difficult to memorize, and practicing day-after-day to make the answers intuitive, and thus, impressive. We are developing heuristics through repeated practice.

There are entire books dedicated to priming and its unconscious effects. Among them are Gladwell's *Blink*, Kahneman's *Thinking, Fast and Slow*, Bargh's *Before You Know It*, and many of Sigmund Freud's works. However, these books merely tell us priming exists. None of them give their readers practical techniques for achieving positive priming. The following chapters in *this* book will do so.

Chapter 10

The How of Visual Absorbent Learning

Thus far, this Part has been devoted to the Why of Visual Absorbent Learning. It is important, however, to plant some seeds in your mind as to How specifically you could go about doing it. This chapter is intentionally short because of how easy it is to do this. Setting yourself up for Visual Absorbent Learning can be done in 5 steps:

1. **Pick your learning subject of choice**. We will go in depth on this a couple pages from now.
2. **Make your subject learnable**. In other words, organize your desired information into a format that can be memorized. This, depending on

the subject, is the hard part.

3. **Print it out**. Depending on your access to a printer and the size of your information, this is a variable cost, but it shouldn't be a big one. Printing on an 8.5 x 11 inch paper will cost you a few cents at an office supply store.
4. **Laminate it if it needs to be waterproof**. If you don't have a laminator, office supply stores offer laminating for under a dollar (depending on size).
5. **Place it in your white space**. To stick my visual learning materials to the fiberglass walls of my shower, I use Command Mounting Strips bought from my local office supply store. You probably need four strips to affix your information to the wall, and a pack of nine strips runs you about 4 bucks. I put up learning materials in my shower over two years ago using Command Strips, and they show no sign of coming down. The strips also work well on normal walls.

There you have it. Think about what you want to learn, make it learnable, and run an errand to the office supply store. If you don't want to do all that work, go to the Visual section at wewanderpurposefully.com. But if you do the work yourself, it costs about five bucks. Five dollars.

FIVE DOLLARS!!!!!!!!!!!!

Here are some things I regularly spend five dollars on:
- One *whole* beer at a bar in Seattle
- Less than *half* of a beer at a Seattle Mariners baseball game

Chapter 11

Activation Energy

Because performing the five steps I've just mentioned is so rare amongst Americans, doing so is seen as taking Visual Absorbent Learning to the extreme. I don't particularly agree with that "extreme" label because the steps are so undemanding. After you complete them, the learning process thereafter is easy too. If only taking Auditory and Experiential Absorbent Learning to the extreme was so easy.

The concept of **activation energy** is the main reason why Visual Absorbent Learning is so simple. Activation energy is supremely important when trying to introduce new habits in your life. Mentioned in chemistry classes, it is defined as the minimum quantity of energy that the reacting species must possess in order to undergo a specific chemical reaction.

I had been exposed to the concept of activation energy during school, but hadn't realized its effect on my daily life until I listened to Shawn Achor's *The Happiness Advantage* while hiking in the Cascade Mountains of Washington.[2] This was an example of a David Foster Wallace fish paradigm shift for me: where (as I discussed in the introduction) the water was everywhere and thus imperceptible. Achor explains this phenomenon as it applies to our daily habits:

> We are drawn — powerfully, magnetically — to those things that are easy, convenient, and habitual, and it is incredibly difficult to overcome this inertia. Active leisure IS more enjoyable, but it almost always requires more initial effort — getting the bike out of the garage, driving to the museum, tuning the guitar, and so on... In physics, activation energy is the initial spark needed to catalyze a reaction. The same energy, both physical and mental, is needed of people to overcome inertia and kickstart a positive habit.

When I woke up after a night's rest on-trail, the hardest thing for me to do was to get out of my cozy sleeping bag, and put on my stinky, wet hiking clothes. This took an enormous effort. Three or four snooze alarms would often pass before I could psych myself up to do it.

Once I summoned enough willpower to complete this first step, packing up camp was easy: I was cold, and the only way to warm myself up would be to keep moving. The reaction could only start moving smoothly once I had mustered the initial jolt of activation energy by getting out of my sleeping bag.

Now, apply the activation energy concept to Visual Absorbent Learning. The initial activation energy needed for Visual Absorbent Learning are the five steps listed in the previous chapter. After that, the convenience of having your

---

[2] To see a picture taken in the Cascades of the most spectacular sunset I've ever seen, go to wewanderpurposefully.com, navigate to the picture menu in the Audiobook section, and click on "Picture 6: Cascade Sunset"

learning materials in your white spaces (places where you expend no additional energy to be) lowers the activation energy of daily Visual Absorbent Learning down to nearly zero. You are already in the spot you need to be, wearing (or not wearing) the clothes you need to wear, and having the necessary equipment in front of you. The remaining energy you need to learn every day is only to lift your head and divert your attention to your Absorbent Learning materials.

Chapter 12

What Should You Learn?

I developed my childhood Chemistry Skill because the periodic table was placed in my white space at a time when I was receptive to learning anything. After childhood, my interests changed. I'm *not* telling you to memorize the periodic table specifically. You can memorize whatever you want. For the majority of my Visual Absorbent Learning engagement as an adult, I've chosen to focus on geography, American history, and linguistics because those topics interest me.

You might not care for geography. You might like pasta, or jokes, or music, or business, or anything else. Guess what? It's *your* life and you can learn about those subjects if you want. You need to make the decision for yourself based on your own self insight and interests.

I once put a list of the Roman Emperors in my shower next to the American Presidents and the world map. I almost never looked at it because I found myself naturally more interested in the other subjects.

In my experience, if you are past childhood, you need to be genuinely interested in a subject to be motivated to study and embrace your Visual Absorbent Learning materials. If you are objectively interested in a subject, you will have lessened the activation energy required to learn even more.

If you like pasta, make or find a labelled picture of the different styles & shapes of pasta. You'll be the pasta maven, able to correctly identify pastas on any authentic Italian menu during date night.

If you like jokes, put up a list of jokes. You'll be able to rattle off dad joke after dad joke, and become the life of the barbeque.

If you like music, put up a list of bands and their members. You'll know who's performing when a song starts playing.

If you like business, put up a list of companies and their respective ticker symbols and CEO's. You'll be able to understand stock analyses and quickly draw your own conclusions.

In order to take advantage of Visual Absorbent Learning, the information you study should be tough to memorize. That's the whole point. You are memorizing things that people don't usually memorize because the act of memorizing those things takes too much time and effort.

Be aware certain subjects naturally don't lend themselves well to Visual Absorbent Learning. I've learned this from experience. Take paintings for example. You could print out some pictures of famous paintings and try to memorize their respective artists, but you'd be limited by the amount of physical space each art piece would populate in your printout.

For example, I could put a bunch of art printouts in my shower, but they would be relatively big, and I would be able to memorize them fairly easily due to their unique natures. I'd immediately be able to memorize Van Gogh's *The Starry Night* because there's nothing else like it. However, *The Starry Night* would still be taking up space in my shower even after I memorized it. For art, the ratio of space-used to learning-opportunity just isn't worth it for me.

See the Visual Absorbent Learning section of wewanderpurposefully.com for more ideas of subjects you could memorize using Visual Absorbent Learning techniques. If you want to lessen the activation energy required for Visual Absorbent Learning even more, purchase some of the graphics for sale there.

As mentioned before, here is what I like to learn with Visual Absorbent Learning:

1. **Geography** - The world map, along with the periodic table, is one of the most effective and succinct purveyors of information of all time. If a normal picture is worth a thousand words, this picture is worth a bajillion words. The ratio of space-used to learning-opportunity is immense. As a bonus, it's readily available for sale online and in multiple outlets, so you wouldn't have to make the map yourself. Remember, Step #2 of how to do Visual Absorbent Learning is to make your information learnable. If you buy a world map for a few bucks, your info is already in a learnable format. Step #2 done. It's also already printed out, and it might even be waterproof already. Voila, Steps #3 and #4 are done too. All you had to do was Step #1 and Step #5: buy the map and put it up.

2. **History** - A timeline of world history would probably be the most useful historical visual learning aid. But that would take up your whole house, as well as all the other houses in your city. There are, however, memorizable lists of important historical figures, like the American Presidents. Knowing a key fact or two about a historical period (e.g. who the President was at a specific time) can be the first stepping stone to more historical knowledge.

3. **Languages** - A person's language (especially if it is an uncommon lan-

guage) is central to their character. There are around 6000 languages in the world. 1000 of them are in New Guinea alone. How many do you know? What are you missing? According to the language learning app Babbel, approximately 360 Million of the 7.53 billion people on Earth speak English as their first and native language. That's under 5% of the planet. What about the other 95%?

Chapter 13

Where and When to Use Visual Absorbent Learning

U p to this point, I've used the action of bathing as an example of white space where Visual Absorbent Learning materials could be placed. If you've ever seen the geeky, marginally-funny sitcom *The Big Bang Theory*, you may have noticed Sheldon and Leonard's shower curtain has the periodic table on it, but that it's facing the wrong way: towards the toilet instead of towards the shower occupant. Perhaps they utilize white space while on the porcelain throne!

If the shower setting doesn't excite you (maybe you have a shower routine that you don't want to mess with, or you like your shower to look simple and uncluttered), or isn't practical for you (say you don't have a compatible shower or you don't have a shower at all), there are loads of other white spaces in which Visual Absorbent Learning could be utilized. Maybe you feel you already use your shower time in a purposeful way. Although a few seconds of learning wouldn't intrude much upon this time, here are some alternative opportunities that could mesh better with your current lifestyle:

1. **Mindless jobs** - Maybe you're selling tickets in a ticket booth, or maybe you're a lawyer stuck in a document review job. Use Visual Absorbent Learning to boost your Sim Income Need Meter and a chosen Skill Meter at the same time.
2. **Hospitals** - If you are a patient in a hospital for an extended period of time and have the use of your consciousness, you could be gaining Skills. Take your mind off of your suffering and suck that lemon dry.
3. **On the fridge** - You need to stand in front of the fridge to satisfy your Hunger Need. Learning could come in the form of a fridge magnet.
4. **Next to the toilet** - You need to visit the toilet to satisfy your Bladder Need. Learning could come in the form of a magazine.
5. **Next to the kitchen sink** - You Need to do the dishes so you don't look like a slob.
6. **Cooking** - You Need to stand in front of the stove while you are cooking.
7. **Folding your laundry** - You Need to fold your laundry (my least favorite chore) so your clothes are wrinkle-free.
8. **Waiting in line** - The mother of all annoying time wasters.
9. **Exercising** - If you are using a stationary bike or treadmill, bring an Absorbent Learning aid (Visual or Auditory) to take your mind off of the grind.
10. **The Back Seat** - Placing Absorbent Learning materials on the back side of the driver or passenger seat makes use of boring commute time, especially for kids.

Here are a few life situations (in no particular order) where Absorbent Learning would be useful:

1. **Trivia Nights** - This may be the first situation you thought of where Visual Absorbent Learning would be useful, and you're totally right. Go out to trivia nights, have some fun, and proudly take home the coveted gift certificates, T-shirts and glassware.
2. **Employee Training** - Company managers should make Absorbent Learning aids new employees can take home with them so they can become effective faster.
3. **Fitness Center Televisions** - Oftentimes, the televisions at fitness centers are showing TV shows or trashy music videos with no sound. Why???
4. **Students** - Law students could put up condensed outlines to help with the Bar Exam. Bartenders could put up mixed drinks and their ingredients for the bartending exam. The list could go on and on.
5. **Prospective Thru-Hikers** - Throw up a map of the trail you want to complete, and start your day by familiarizing yourself with the trail to get remotivated.
6. **Politicians** - A person's ability to get elected largely depends on how popular that person is. If a person has more weak ties than their political opponent, they are much more likely to win the election. Weak ties not only vote for people they consider to be their weak ties, but they also influence their own family and friends to vote similarly.
7. **Prisons** - If you are a convict, and the prison you find yourself in is cooperative, this can be the ultimate example of white space. Spend your time improving yourself for your eventual release.
8. **Lead Singers** - I am a notorious lyrical forgetter. If I used Visual Absorbent Learning, I wouldn't have to embarrassingly resort to bee-bop scatting when lyrics escape me.

Chapter 14

Punch Your Card

"Today's society wants to skip the process. I hate that. Do the little things right to reach the big goals."

—TOM IZZO

Patience is the key to Absorbent Learning. The fruits of Absorbent Learning may not show up right away, but sooner or later the threshold will be reached where the knowledge you've acquired becomes useful in relational situations. In the meantime, you haven't hurt anything by knowing a few apparently trivial facts.

A motivating example you can look to comes from the world of physics. Solzhenitsyn described it well in *The Gulag Archipelago*:

> Physics is aware of phenomena that occur only at threshold magni-

tudes, which do not exist at all until a certain threshold, encoded by forces unknown to nature, has been crossed... you can cool oxygen to 100 degrees below 0 Centigrade and exert as much pressure as you want. It does not yield but remains a gas. But as soon as -183 degrees is reached, it liquefies and begins to flow.

Apprenticeships, voice lessons, construction projects, and college degrees all require years of service to eventually (if they ever) become useful. Absorbent Learning could also potentially take years to become useful. Like anything worth striving for, it is not an instant magical elixir. Learn one thing at a time and eventually the whole knowledge set will be useful to you. You could memorize how to say "thank you" in Greek ("*efcharistó*") today, and serendipitously meet someone who speaks Greek tomorrow. Or you might meet your first Greek ten years from now.

Nevertheless, learning the first few tidbits of information motivates you to keep learning the information until you have learned it all. Legendary basketball coach John Wooden provided this nugget of wisdom:

> When you improve a little each day, eventually big things occur... Don't look for the quick, big improvement. Seek the small improvement one day at a time. That's the only way it happens — and when it happens, it lasts.

Say you memorize Martin Van Buren was the eighth President of the United States. You now are more likely to continue your presidential knowledge by memorizing William Henry Harrison as the ninth.

Moreover, while listening to Dan and Chip Heath's book called *Switch* near Lake Tahoe[3], I heard about a deviously clever business tactic employed

---
3   To see a picture of the woods west of Lake Tahoe during the golden hour, go to wewanderpurposefully.com, navigate to the picture menu in the Audiobook section, and click on "Picture 7: Tahoe Woods"

by stores who give out punchcards to their customers. Let's say a sandwich store gives you a punchcard, and you receive punches for every sub sandwich you purchase. After the tenth punch, you get a free sub. Posing as a generous customer perk, these stores regularly give customers the punchcards with two "free" punches already punched.

Scientific studies, however, conclude a person is much more likely to buy eight sandwiches to finish out a ten sandwich punchcard than to start at zero punches and finish a punchcard that required only eight sandwich purchases.

Start your learning and you will be more motivated to finish your punchcard.

As we End Part 2, here are some takeaway Action Items for Visual Absorbent Learning:
- Reflect upon your learning goals.
- Choose what you want to learn. See the visual section of wewanderpurposefully.com for suggestions and products.
- Identify a white space location.
- Make or buy a visual memorization aide, and place it in your white space.
- Look at it everyday. Put in the effort to memorize it.
- Follow @etrav_learning on social media and join the Absorbent Learning newsletter for continual inspiration.

PART 3

Experiential Absorbent Learning:
A Farewell to Comfort

Chapter 15

The Sims and You, Part Deux

Experiential Absorbent Learning is all about attuning yourself to another point of view, and creating a responsible moral compass to aid the application of your learning. In this section, we will explore two ways to participate in Experiential Absorbent Learning: experiencing different activities and experiencing different places.

To illustrate the value of experiencing different activities, let's revisit *The Sims*.

As your Sim progresses in their career, another determinant slows progression to the next level. To be promoted, you need to satisfy not only the Skills prerequisites, but also the "Friend" prerequisite. For example, to progress along the political career track to become a Level 10 Mayor of SimCity, you need to be "Friends" with 17 other Sims. To foster friendships with other Sims in SimCity, you need to spend time and interact with them. When doing so, a relationship meter for the two interacting Sims appears above your Sim's head. The more you pleasantly interact with the other Sim, the higher the meter goes. Once you reach the friend threshold on the meter, you then become "Friends" with the other Sim. The Sims you positively interact with most frequently are shoo-ins to count towards your career friend requirement as your "Best Friends."

You then need to target random Sims from SimCity you haven't interacted with yet to gain new friendships (and satisfy the career Friends Prerequisite). The two most effective commands your Sim could use when attempting to befriend another Sim are "Talk" and "Joke."

When you talk and joke with the other Sim, pictograms of objects, like a soccer ball or a fishing net, appear above your Sim's head to indicate the subject of the conversation. You could spend about fifteen minutes of gameplay queueing up Talk and Joke commands for your Sim, and cross the friend threshold with the targeted Sim fairly quickly. That Sim would then count towards your career's Friend requirement. Conversely, if you spent a lengthy amount of time away from the Sim you had previously become friends with, your relationship meter slowly drains until you fall below the Friend threshold. You are no longer friends with that Sim; you need to spend more time with them to rekindle the friendship and have it count towards your career ambitions.

Again, I can't help but notice parallels between the way Sims make friends and the way real people make friends. Even in a world where social media has slackened the definition of friendship down towards the acquaintance level, the way to make friends in real life is by interacting positively with them (namely talking and joking).

Likewise, anyone who has cultivated a nascent friendship recognizes the need to keep spending time with the newfound friend in order to maintain the friendship.

Even the Friend Prerequisite echoes reality. It's essentially a networking requirement. The more people you know, the easier it may be to land a job or promotion. To quote an overused but unfortunately accurate adage: "It's not what you know, it's *who* you know."

Additionally, your brand new Sim friend counts as much towards your Friend Prerequisite as your Sim's best friend. In reality, networking works much the same way. The person outside your immediate best friend circle (a weak tie) can hook you up with a job just as quickly as your best friend can.

Furthermore, the random pictograms of common interests that pop up during the Sims' interactions (the soccer balls and fishing nets) mirror the fluid nature of conversations we have with weak ties in real life. When you know virtually nothing about someone, any conversation subject will be enlightening for your young friendship. If the conversation turns towards interests, then it would behoove you to be conversant about different things. And the more things you can converse about intelligently, the more likely you will find a common interest with your conversation partner. You are now more likely to positively bond with this person. This is the driving force behind the sociological heuristic phenomenon known as homophily. Kathryn Schulz, in her book *Being Wrong*, describes homophily quite well:

> Ancient epicureans, orthodox Jews, socialists, suffragists, indie rockers in skinny jeans, all of them… sought out and, when possible, settled among the like-minded. Sociologists call this predilection: homophily, the tendency to like people who are like us… [M]ost of us live around people who look, earn, worship, and vote a whole lot like we do. As the Washington Post pointed out after the 2008 Presidential election, nearly half of all Americans live in landslide counties where Democrats or Republicans regularly win in a rout.

We can take advantage of humanity's innate preference to be around like-minded people by forcing ourselves to be like-minded with as many people as possible. We can do this by leaving our comfort zones and varying the activities we enjoy. Whether it's going to a cooking class, taking tennis lessons, running a 5K, taking improv comedy classes, participating in a book club, taking a dance class, learning to play an instrument, or anything else: the choice is up to you. The more activities you engage in, the more people you attune with.

Experiential Absorbent Learning, like hiking the PCT when you don't like hiking, supplies you with more conversation topics to exploit homophily. Any mutual connection you can form with your conversant is useful for growing the young relationship quicker. These connections get you closer to the Friend Threshold *faster*. Closer to the point where your conversation partner becomes a useful networking connection, or weak tie, for your personal life and your career.

Chapter 16

I Eat Too Much

Personally, I oftentimes vary my activities with exercise in mind. I like to multitask. If I Need to exercise, I might as well benefit from Experiential Absorbent Learning while I'm at it. In recent years, my exercising has been taken to the extreme because of a troublesome habit stemming from my childhood.

Being part of a troop of five, hungry, football-playing brothers, my mom had her hands full trying to keep our stomachs full. Preferring to feed her kids with wholesome foods that did not include the unhealthy snacks they loved, my mother had turned "snacks" into an entity loudly requested, but rarely received.

On the infrequent occasion my mom would bring home snacks to eat, a typically calm household was transformed into a vicious free-for-all feeding frenzy straight out of Shark Week. If, by some miracle, mom brought home a deluxe pack of Goldfish, you had better scarf down as many as you could as quickly as you could. Otherwise, as my dad would say, "You snooze, you lose."

The snacks would be gone in minutes. I sometimes would visit friends' houses and be overwhelmed at the sight of whole pantries full of Goldfish, Cheez-its (my favorite), Ruffles, Chips Ahoy, Pretzels, Wheat Thins, and Doritos; havens of forbidden fruit that, if they were to exist at our house, would have been greedily consumed like Spongebob shoveling down Krabby Patties ten at a time.

On one memorable occasion, unbeknownst to my brothers, my mom came home from the supermarket with groceries for the week. I helped her bring all the groceries into the house, but noticed a rarity amongst the booty. There it was: a 48 pack of delectable Fruit by the Foot Fruit-Roll-ups, the Holy Grail of snacks. Jackpot. I surreptitiously smuggled the loot to an enclosed space, and I immediately proceeded to eat all 48 of them.

Since those days, it has been a constant struggle to keep my eating habits in check. Due to wallowsome desk-job-induced sloth, I steadily gained forty pounds over the three years ensuing college. By the time I started the PCT, I had ballooned to a cumbersome 241 pounds. At my height, I had a Body Mass Index (BMI) of 33.5, making me technically obese.

Secondary to listening to audiobooks, one of my reasons for hiking the PCT was to whip myself back in shape. I took a physical before my hike so I could have a baseline to track my health progress. After routine blood tests, I received a panicked call from my doctor telling me I needed to go back to his office to take more tests because my liver enzyme counts were alarmingly high. As he explained to me, when there is inflammation of the liver, the liver cells rupture, die, and release the enzymes contained within them (known as ALT and AST enzymes) into the bloodstream. Thus, if many liver cells are dying, there are higher elevations of ALT and AST detected when blood tests are performed.

I hurriedly got an ultrasound done hours before my departure, and hopped on my flight from Seattle to Southern California without knowing the results. A few days into the hike, I was relieved to be informed the elevated numbers were not the result of a cancer or other chthonic ailment, but due to the presence of an abnormally high amount of fat within my liver.

Five months and many miles later, I took another round of blood tests to compare my liver numbers from before trail to those after trail.

I went from 129 to 22 (an 83% improvement) in the ALT test of which 50 is the upper healthy limit, and from 52 to 19 (a 64% improvement) in the AST test of which 35 is the upper healthy limit.

I finished the trail at a slim 189 pounds — a 52 pound loss over 5 months.[1] I had actually lost 52 pounds within the first 100 days, whereafter my weight loss plateaued. It turns out that walking all day and not overeating (because food is heavy) is a good weight loss program. I was no longer obese, but I was still quote-unquote "overweight" with a 26.5 BMI (I'm not sure how much more these BMI people want from me).

There is nary a positive to be found where overeating is concerned, other than the short term pleasure stemming from it. This pleasure is attributable to the chemical neurotransmitter known as dopamine.

Dopamine naturally occurs in the brain, and is responsible for the pleasurable feelings we get when we laugh, or receive a notification on our phone. Certain drugs like cocaine and ecstasy are designed to manipulate dopamine transmission in the body (hence the narcotic nickname "dope"). Too much exposure to this heightening of dopamine levels causes a reliance upon it. We call this reliance addiction.

---

[1] To see comparative mirror selfies illustrating the effect of a 52 pound loss on my upper body, go to wewanderpurposefully.com, navigate to the picture menu in the Audiobook section, and click on "Picture 8: Fat and Hairy Erics"

Chapter 17

Cognitive Dissonance

In my life, I have decided to give into my overeating habit many times, willingly choosing to indulge my addiction. During these times, there were two competing statements at war within my mind:

Contradictory Statement #1: Overeating is bad.
Contradictory Statement #2: I am overeating.

I never knew it at the time, but I was experiencing what is known in behavioral psychology as **cognitive dissonance**.

Cognitive dissonance is everywhere. It is defined as the uncomfortable sensation occurring when two contradictory ideas are present within your mind. It occurs most often when someone's behavior is inconsistent with their beliefs or feelings.

It is the mental battle that raged in my mind every day on the PCT.

Contradictory Statement #1: I don't want to hike right now.
Contradictory Statement #2: I'm hiking right now.

I had never thought deeply about cognitive dissonance until I listened to *Being Wrong* by Kathryn Schulz while engulfed in wildfire smoke in Northern California.[2] I had a vague understanding of cognitive dissonance, but had never given it much thought. I soon realized cognitive dissonance permeated my life at every turn. This realization was yet another example of a personal David Foster Wallace fish-water paradigm shift.

Cognitive dissonance underlies our life's most impactful decisions. This concept will thus be a recurring reference throughout the remainder of this book. As I'll explain later, Experiential Absorbent Learning is the one variable *we can control* that can aid our decision making in situations of personal cognitive dissonance.

Leon Festinger, godfather of the cognitive dissonance concept, described methods to overcome the two warring thoughts in your mind. One way in which to do this is to add more thoughts to the battle.

Say you work at a job, but you hate that job. Boom! Cognitive dissonance. If you add another thought, say, "I do awesome stuff on the weekends to make up for my terrible job" or "I only have to do this job for another few months until my mixtape drops," your mental battle would rage less violently.

The driving force behind cognitive dissonance is the factor of choice. You are *choosing* to contradict yourself.

---

[2] To see a picture of the trail disappearing into wildfire haze, go to wewanderpurposefully.com, navigate to the picture menu in the Audiobook section, and click on "Picture 9: Wildfire Haze"

Not being a doctor (other than my prestigious PCT PhD), I would venture to assert the committal of this conscious choice is the root cause of depression. If you had a choice between doing work that you loved, but chose (because of financial or convenience incentives) to work at a job that you hate, then you will have introduced the war of cognitive dissonance into your life. If, on the other hand, you are born into a situation where you have no choice but to work in an unsavory job, you would not be feeling those same feelings of dissonance.

The American Dream, the belief that you can choose your own path and work your way to stardom, is what makes this country amazing. It also, ironically, places America among the top most depressed nations in the world.

To combat and compensate for the cognitive dissonance I feel after overeating, I over-exercise. By doing this, I am adding a third thought to my mental battle:

Contradictory Statement #3: I will overexercise to offset my overeating.

If you burn as many calories as you ingest, you will stay at around the same weight. If I was sufficiently motivated to lose weight, I would eat healthy all the time and still over-exercise. As many can attest, this is easier said than done. Nevertheless, I regularly make the decision to do extreme exercise activities so I can indulge my overeating addiction. When choosing these activities I try to do things that force me to exit my comfort zone. By doing this, I am ascribing to Experiential Absorbent Learning. I Need to exercise so I might as well benefit from Absorbent Learning while I'm at it.

Chapter 18

Hiking 101

An extreme example of Experiential Absorbent Learning is to hike the PCT. It is the epitome of being physically uncomfortable. You suffer through injury-riddled days without a bed, without a shower, without a toilet, without prepared meals, covered in sweat and dirt, dealing with aches and blisters, soaking wet from the rain, burned from the sun, frozen from the snow, choked by wildfire smoke, hiking and hitchhiking with strangers, hemorrhaging money, swarmed by flies, eaten alive by mosquitoes, and terrified of random animal noises during pitch black night-hikes. You act like a homeless vagrant, while embarking on an odyssey the equivalent of 101 marathons (2,650 miles) through deserts and over mountains. All with a heavy ruck on your back. It is uncomfortable. That is the point.

First and foremost, the trail is a mental challenge of making the uncomfortable comfortable.

The idea of "comfort" itself is purely a mental creation. The people of Siberia are comfortable with negative degree temperatures because they are used to it. They have transformed their relatively uncomfortable situation into a more comfortable one. Transport a Floridian to Siberia and I will show you an unhappy and uncomfortable Floridian. But, guess what? If that Floridian spends enough time in Siberia, they will eventually *become* a Siberian, and will find themselves to be comfortable while freezing.

The PCT is the same thing. Throw a guy named Eric from Orange County (essentially one humongous city conjoined with Los Angeles) into the wilderness, and he will have some growing pains. But, he will eventually force himself into a new comfort zone.

Hiking is an activity rewarding determination and endurance, more than talent or vanity muscles. After mastering the mental challenges, conquering the physical challenges of the trail naturally follow.

You can, however, get unlucky. You could take a bad step on one of the tens of thousands of steps you took that day and break your leg. I've witnessed stories like this myself. Just like that, no matter what your mental foundation consisted of, your thru-hike comes to a sudden, devastating conclusion. After mental breakdowns, this unluckiness is a main reason why there is only a reported 20-30% success rate for PCT aspirants fulfilling their ultimate goals of crossing the finish line in Canada.

There were plenty of times when I tripped on a rock, or slipped in mud, and fell on my face. I rolled my ankle countless times. But I was never left with a debilitating injury. Seeing intrepid hikers more capable than myself fail has been one of the saddest tribulations I've ever witnessed. Their spirits were so visibly vibrant, yet their body let them down. These people are not weak. It could have happened to me many times, but fortunately did not. I am reminded of my favorite Teddy Roosevelt quotation contained within his speech entitled *The Man in the Arena*:

> It is not the critic who counts; not the man who points out how the strong man stumbles, or where the doer of deeds could have done them better. The credit belongs to the man who is actually in the arena, whose face is marred by dust and sweat and blood; who strives valiantly; who errs, who comes short again and again, because there is no effort without error and shortcoming; but who does actually strive to do the deeds; who knows great enthusiasms, the great devotions; who spends himself in a worthy cause; who at the best knows in the end the triumph of high achievement, and who at the worst, if he fails, at least fails while daring greatly, so that his place shall never be with those cold and timid souls who neither know victory nor defeat.

The hiker community surrounding the PCT is chock-full of superheroes who dare to push the limits of their comfort zones.

When you attach yourself to a community, you take on all the stereotypical baggage associated with that community. The mind's unconscious usage of stereotypes is another example of fast, heuristic thinking.

Another reason I was drawn to the PCT is how I viewed the stereotypes associated with PCT hikers. The trail seemed to be a venerable goal to me. Theodore Roosevelt also said: "Nothing in the world is worth having or worth doing unless it means effort, pain, difficulty.... I have never in my life envied a human being who led an easy life."

We as a society tend to allocate more admiration and respect to people who have dealt with and overcome hardships. We count Abraham Lincoln and Franklin Roosevelt among our best presidents precisely because of their leadership during times of hardship and crisis.

We respect people who have gone through hardship, but we cannot control how much hardship we are subjected to when we are children. I listened to Malcolm Gladwell's *David And Goliath* while hiking through misty mountains on my way into Cascade Locks.[3]

Gladwell mentions the challenges of a man who started from nothing, struck it rich, and *then* raised his children:

> He had children that he loved very dearly. Like any parent, he wanted to provide for them. To give them more than he had. But he had created a giant contradiction and he knew it. He was successful because he had learned the long and hard way about the value of money, and the meaning of work, and the joy and fulfillment that come from making your own way in the world. But because of his success, it would be difficult for his children to learn those same lessons. Children of multi-millionaires in Hollywood do not rake the leaves of their neighbors in Beverly Hills, their fathers do not wave the electricity bill angrily at them if they leave the lights on. They do not sit in a basketball arena behind a pillar and wonder what it would be like to sit courtside. They live courtside.

Due partially to my parent's hard work, and partially from our family's inheritance, I grew up in a family squarely placed on the upper edges of middle class.

My childhood was fantastic. I experienced little undue hardship. Through pure chance, my race (white), sex (male), and orientation (heterosexual) aligns with long entrenched American societal advantages. I'm complaining about overeating snack food (first world problems!!!), when many less fortunate chil-

---

[3] To see a picture of a mist covered valley near Cascade Locks, go to wewanderpurposefully.com, navigate to the picture menu in the Audiobook section, and click on "Picture 10: Misty Mountains"

dren are underfed in general.

Cognitive dissonance alert:

Contradictory Statement #1: I reaped all the rewards of a well-provided and unworried childhood.
Contradictory Statement #2: I personally did nothing to earn those rewards.

Another way to combat the uncomfortable nature of cognitive dissonance is to diminish the significance of one of your conflicting thoughts. Like many do, you could choose to diminish Statement #2. You could say to yourself it's no big deal you didn't earn any of your rewards.

Alternatively, you could choose to rectify one of your competing statements. For example, you could choose to rectify Statement #1 by casting away your possessions and rewards.

Another option, the one I subconsciously ended up choosing myself by hiking the PCT, is to rectify Statement #2 — you could introduce hardship into your life to feel as if you are earning your rewards.

Not everyone feels the need to create genuine hardship and introduce real fear into their life. But doing so makes you an unambiguously more interesting person (to yourself anyways).

Fortunately, there are ways to artificially introduce genuine hardship without actually destroying your way of life or discarding your possessions.

One way to accomplish this is to choose to do something like the PCT. By purposely introducing hardship into your life, you not only add to the list of people you may attune with, but you also garner respect for yourself and from others.

Henry David Thoreau's move to Walden Pond, Chris McCandless' death in

Alaska, Huckleberry Finn's journey down the Mississippi River with Jim, Jon Snow's expeditions north of the Wall: these are all stories, real or fictional, that have been written because their subjects experience hardship. These stories are unique and worth writing about.

Are *you* worth writing about?

Whether the challenge be physical, intellectual, financial, or otherwise, you can choose *inherently challenging* hobbies and activities. Watching TV is not challenging. No one is impressed to hear you've binge-watched every season of *The Office* on Netflix (which I've admittedly done). All you needed to do was drop a few bucks on a Netflix subscription, and not move for hours on end.

By challenging yourself, you are redefining the physical and mental limitations you've unwittingly preset.

For example, a few years ago, I completed my first and only marathon in Couer d'Alene, Idaho. I jogged the first half, limped the second half, and finished the race in 5 hours and 46 minutes. Not a respectable time, but I at least reached the end fourteen minutes before they tore down the finish line. I was helplessly bedridden for a whole day afterwards. At that point, I could not have dreamed that towards the end of the PCT, I'd regularly complete marathon days with a 40 pound ruck, and, at one point, hike the equivalent of 15 marathons in 15 consecutive days. [4]

---

4   To see a picture of my Apple health app showing 15 marathons walked in 15 days, go to wewanderpurposefully.com, navigate to the picture menu in the Audiobook section, and click on "Picture 11: 15 Marathons in 15 days"

Chapter 19

Tips for Leaving your Comfort Zone

I know it's hard to leave your comfort zone. Comfort is easy. We all seek shortcuts to comfort. Some people are limited as to how they can leave their comfort zones due to physical restraints. Those people are forced to be more creative. Regardless, there are a couple techniques that you can use to help yourself leave your comfort zone.

First, tell the people around you that you're going to do it, whatever "it" may be (in my case, a bike race, a marathon, or a mountain summit attempt). Do this before you even begin to train or put any money down on your escapades. In doing so, you introduce a measure of self-induced peer pressure, and thus shoehorn a sense of social accountability into your mindset.

Jon Krakauer's experience on the Devil's Thumb in Alaska, as told in his book, *Into the Wild*, describes this peer pressure you should purposely seek:

> My escapade on the north face had rattled me, and I didn't want to go up on the Thumb again at all. But the thought of returning to Boulder in defeat, wasn't very appealing, either. I could all too easily picture the smug expression of condolence I'd receive from those who'd been certain of my failure from the get-go.

The more people you tell, the more people you would seemingly disappoint and prove right if you didn't go through with it.

After telling people about your plans, you may then proceed to put your money where your mouth is.

If you are going to ride a bike race, you need to buy a bike, a helmet, some bike shoes, and register for the race itself. Not cheap. You supply the activation energy needed to begin training by buying all the equipment before you even start training. Now, if you didn't train, you'd not only be misinforming your friends, but you'd also be wasting money.

The more monetary capital and social capital that you invest in an event or experience, the more motivated you are to start training. The more likely you are to actually go through with *attempting* the event or experience. An attempt is also an admirable feat. I repeat: **Diminished experience is better than non-experience**.

Exit your comfort zone. Every time you do, you become something else. It literally builds character.

If you were a character in a novel, how long would it take the author to describe you? Are there only a couple words needed to describe you and your quirks?

Every time you exit your comfort zone, you become something else. If you climb a mountain, you become a mountain climber. If you take guitar lessons, you become a guitarist. By doing so, you open yourself up to a whole new group of weak ties. You put more tools in your toolbox, so to speak.

For example, I can now talk to other writers, and know exactly what it's like to be in their shoes. I couldn't have known the writer's struggle, and thus couldn't have been able to connect deeply with other writers, had I not become one myself. Discouraging (sometimes necessary) realists will tell aspiring writers that "there are many writers in the world."

I'm now more attuned to all of them.

Chapter 20

Bursting the Bubble

"I learned more about happiness during my travels to Africa and the Middle East in the midst of a crisis than in twelve years of sheltered study."

—SHAWN ACHOR, THE HAPPINESS ADVANTAGE

Throughout Part 3 so far, I have stressed how engaging in activities out of your comfort zone stimulates your growth as a person. Now, we will delve into the importance of getting out of your existing bubble and traveling to different places. Your comfort zone is not only your daily routine, but also the place you reside, and the customs involved therein.

Never in history has it been this easy to travel. Traveling is no longer esoteric. People do it all the time. Because of this, it's never been more advantageous to attune yourself to others. Not only are we able to travel to an alarming amount of places, people from those places can now come and visit us. Before recent advances, there was little incentive for this type of attunement. We encountered those of different perspectives infrequently.

The amount of places someone has travelled is essentially a function of how many opportunities he or she has had to travel. Most times, it is a gift to be able to travel. I've been lucky enough to travel to 48 states and 40 countries, and almost every single one of these opportunities has been a gift.

As I've mentioned before, I grew up in a decently well-off family. But with five eternally hungry boys and five college tuitions, our family vacations were not typically of the international, or even interstate, variety.

Outside of family vacations, my first travels were Asian and North American tours with my childhood choir. I was invited to participate in these tours because I was well-behaved and a good enough singer. That said, I still was only able to go because my parents could pay for the travel costs.

My point is, there will always be someone who travels more than you. For that matter, there will always be someone doing more extreme things than you. I hiked a ridiculous amount of miles from Mexico to Canada in 156 days, but there are people who do "yo-yo" hikes of the PCT in the same amount of time: they hike from Mexico to Canada and then *back down* to Mexico. Ridiculousness is clearly a relative measure.

It is important to realize, however, that where, and how often you travel is not as important as *how* you travel.

You could get the all-inclusive resort package to Tahiti and spend your vacation with your significant other in a yurt over the turquoise water. That sounds fun, but you could also do something similar without flying all the way to Tahiti. Conversely, if you went to Tahiti and spent time with the locals, intentionally observing their customs in a candid fashion, your trip to Tahiti would be worthwhile and serve a *purpose*. You would have a glimpse of what it's like to be a Tahitian. You'd be on your first steps to *becoming* Tahitian.

You could also go to a new place and act obnoxiously, perpetuating America's worst stereotypes.

Alternatively, you can do as the Romans do, absorb your surroundings, and sponge up the unique aspects of where you find yourself. Through my travels I have noticed if you treat others with respect, they will treat you with respect.

I've had beers and amazing conversations with friendly German, Russian, and Japanese people in their home countries. In my dad's lifetime, we have been mortal enemies with these countries. Just 75 years later, I'm laughing and joking with them with thoughts of war and nationalism far removed from our minds. I've watched the Olympics and World Cup games in different countries, and been amazed at the camaraderie displayed by all.

When more travelers begin acting in this way, we can begin to rewrite our stereotypes.

Furthermore, if you see, taste, or hear things you are unfamiliar with, ask questions. Ralph Waldo Emerson said: "Every man I meet is my superior in some way. In that, I learn of him." Have the humility to admit your own ignorance. In doing so, you open yourself up to new avenues of knowledge.

When you observe a culture in its authentic, candid state, you begin to understand how that culture functions in relation to your own. The culture could be on the other side of the world, or it could be the next town over. When you experience it, you begin to understand what makes their culture different from yours. You suddenly are granted the context to be able to imagine walking a mile in their shoes (if they have any shoes to begin with).

These are the beginnings of empathy: the most important quality a person can gain or display.

Chapter 21

Escape Room

Warning: this chapter contains adult subject material

"I don't believe in your stinky world!"

— JACK, ROOM

In 2015, the movie *Room*, starring Brie Larson (who went on to win a Best Actress Oscar for her role) and child actor Jacob Tremblay, hit theaters.

The story is told by a five-year-old boy named Jack (played by Tremblay) who lives in Room with Ma (played by Larson). Also in Room is Bed, Toilet, Wardrobe, and an assortment of other household items. What makes Room special is that all these supposedly common household items are not common at all. In fact, there is only one of these items known in existence (at least to Jack), and thus each is referred to in the Capital.

It dawns on the audience that, as far as Jack knows, nothing exists outside of Room. It is slowly revealed his mother has been kidnapped and imprisoned inside an impenetrable soundproof garden shed by a man named Old Nick for seven years. During this time, he has continually sexually assaulted her, thus resulting in the pregnancy that eventually became Jack. Ma, fearing Jack's reaction, chooses not to tell Jack about the outside world. Instead, Jack is indoctrinated with the notion that the whole world consists of Room.

Upon Jack's fifth birthday, it becomes clear to Ma the living situation will eventually become untenable. Jack must escape Room.

What happens next is exquisitely portrayed. Ma tries to explain to Jack how the world actually is, that the world is much bigger than Room and there are many more Beds and Sinks and Toilets in existence. This goes against all Jack has ever thought or experienced. Jack naturally resists, berating Ma and screaming "Liar, liar, pants on fire!" We are then witness to an ingenious scheme of escape in which much of the outcome's success relies almost entirely on how Jack will react to things he has never seen before (like grass or the sky).

As a metaphor for Jack's situation, it is helpful to compare the biological differences between **bays** and **estuaries**.

There are two types of water that occupy bodies of water: saltwater and freshwater. A bay consists of only saltwater. An estuary mixes both types of water, saltwater and freshwater. San Francisco Bay, since it is fed by both freshwater rivers originating from snow melt in the Sierra Nevada Mountain Range[5] and by saltwater from the Pacific Ocean, should technically be called San Fran-

---
5 To see me and Eddie covering Led Zeppelin's Bron-Y-Aur Stomp with Eddie's guitar and my bear cannister near Mammoth in the Sierra Nevada Mountains, go to wewanderpurposefully.com, navigate to the picture menu in the Audiobook section, and click on "Picture 12: Mammoth Stomp"

cisco Estuary. Estuaries are especially vibrant ecosystems with the ability to house species normally restricted to either freshwater or saltwater. Accordingly, estuaries are home to striking biodiversity not found anywhere else in the world. Many of the most populous locations on the planet lie just a few miles from an estuary. The Nile Delta, Puget Sound, Chesapeake Bay, Rio de la Plata, the Thames estuary, and many more. All are examples of estuaries.

Jack existed in the most extreme of bays. Room was composed of pure saltwater.

There were no outside influences to affect Jack. Thus, he was completely unaware of the world outside of Room. He grew up with one viewpoint, the one the immediate surroundings he was born into provided him. He existed in his own unique paradigm of influences and experiences.

When he left Room, he discovered the ways of his childhood were not the only ways of the world. Jack, through his escape, experienced what others see. Before leaving Room, Jack was incapable of seeing the world through someone else's point of view. He could not begin to fathom other points of view because he had no knowledge of them and had not experienced them himself.

By virtue of his new experiences, he cultivated a trickle of fresh water that permeated his prior conceptions of reality. He turned part of his bay into an estuary.

The limits of our own experiences often insulate our minds from the possibility of empathizing with different perspectives. Therefore, to have the ability to empathize with those whose backgrounds differ from our own, we need to expand our own realms of experience.

Seeing other people's point of view can be aptly portrayed with the concept of **parallax** (the adjective form of parallax is **parallactic**). Used in modern times as common terminology in the photography and astronomy worlds, I first happened upon parallax while listening to James Joyce's *Ulysses* as I crossed into snowy Canada. Parallax is defined as the displacement, or difference, in the apparent position of an object viewed along two different lines of sight. It is seeing two apparently contradictory things at the same time. Rooted from the Greek, it is related to the word paradox (two contradictory truths existing at the same time).

The following quote will put parallax into an understandable format:

> To get your own personal idea of parallax, hold your right hand up in front of your face. Stick up your... finger and then close your left eye. Without moving your finger, close your right eye and then open your left. Go back and forth, back and forth, and you'll realize that it seems like your finger is moving. As your vision switches from one eye to another and back again, your finger seems to be displaced. This is a small and simple example of a parallax.

That quote is from a website called Shmoop. Normally I wouldn't cite something called Shmoop, but nothing in *Ulysses* ever made any sense.

Recognizing how people can 1) simultaneously have different perspectives originating from their unique backgrounds, and 2) therefore react differently to an issue, is paramount for a respectful society.

By thinking in a parallactic way, you can now fathom both sides of an argument as simultaneously true and simultaneously real. The realization of parallax expands your own personal paradigm manyfold by adding others' paradigms to it.

Parallax turns your bays... into estuaries.

Chapter 22

Exiting the Bay

"If I cannot change when the circumstances demand it, how can I expect others to?"

— **NELSON MANDELA**, INVICTUS

Taking a candid look at your own life can result in the discovery of bays. Just like a paradigm shift, they are imperceptible until you notice and confront them for the first time.

Upon reflection of my own experiences, it has become clear to me that my childhood consisted of several bays. One of which was the avoidance of all things homosexual. In fact, the entire subject of sexuality (hetero or homo) was stymied well into my teens, likely due to the perceived uncomfortability of the subject. These years of silence regarding sexuality led me to seek influence elsewhere to fill in the gaps myself.

I imagine many American kids in my generation grew up this way.

My family was very heteronormative. I was surrounded by macho-ness everywhere I turned. Football, maybe the most outwardly heteronormative of sports, was a constant theme in my life. My family was Catholic, but didn't expressly espouse the traditional views of the Church. We were never anti-gay, but homosexuality was most definitely not the norm. It was somewhat taboo — a subject largely omitted and rarely discussed. Because of this sheltered aspect of my childhood, I was in a bay.

When someone in my life came out as gay, I looked upon the revelation not as a personal defect, but, more than anything else, as *weird*. I felt this way because I was never particularly close to anyone who had come out as gay. I was never forced to confront my prior conceptions, or lackthereof, until I was 24 years old.

After 24 years of being largely sheltered from homosexuality, my hiking partner Eddie's identical twin brother, Luke, came out as gay.

Suddenly, I had to come to terms with my own heuristic preconceptions towards homosexuality. When I moved to Seattle after college, Eddie and Luke's family had become a fixture in my life. When my own family was a few states away, I would spend holidays with Eddie and Luke as an honorary member of their family. They are beyond welcoming, and I am extremely grateful for their presence in my life.

When I left for the PCT, I still had not taken the time to understand and learn about Luke and his sexuality. Along my hike, it became readily apparent to me I needed to rethink any heuristic prejudice I had stemming from the limits of my own experience.

David Foster Wallace's fish struck yet again: I discovered I dwelt in a bay on the subject of homosexuality. I confronted the fact that my childhood was not perfect. No one's is.

Luke is a brave soul to come out to his (also very heteronormative and traditional) family. He is emblematic of all those who have had to come out to their own friends and families, whether they were accepted for their sexuality or not. These people are brave for being true to who they are, but they are not the *only* ones who need to be brave for society to accept homosexuality as a norm.

To change global norms on sexuality, the ones who also need to be brave are children (like myself), who are born into bays — inoculated by the paradigm where gay men and women are weird, different, or undesirable. These children have parents or guardians who either explicitly denounced homosexuality, or avoided the subject entirely.

In her book *Being Wrong*, Kathryn Schulz discusses children and their upbringings:

> Children believe in things like Santa Claus and the tooth fairy not because they are particularly credulous, but for the same reasons the rest of us believe our beliefs. Their information about these phenomena comes from trusted sources (typically, their parents) and is often supported by physical evidence (cookie crumbs by the chimney, quarters under the pillow). It isn't the kids' fault that the evidence is fabricated and that their sources mislead them. Nor is it their fault that their primary community, outside of their family, generally consists of other children, who tend to be equally ill-informed.

As Schulz points out, we are primed from childhood, and we are primed by the only people that matter to us: the trusted sources of our upbringing.

The anti-gay lobby is full of people who refuse to see homosexuality as acceptable. They choose instead to categorically dislike all gay people.

Here is my point: if you are pro-gay, and choose to look at anti-gay people through an empathetic, parallactic lens (a lens that sees from their point of view of how, and why, they came to misunderstand or detest homosexuality), you cease to see them as intrinsically wicked. They become victims of circumstance. They are not evil for thinking the way they do. They simply were primed as children to think a certain way. That way naturally became a habit and frame of mind. Their bay is still completely saltwater.

In *Room*, Jack was only able to exit his bay because Ma, his one and only influence, was the person convincing him to change his point of view. In the real world, your biggest initial influences rarely change their points of view, thus making it difficult to exit your bay. You must take the initiative to detach yourself from singular influences. You have a responsibility to force yourself to develop into an estuary.

Take an unbiased look at your own life.

Could it be possible *you* live in a bay on certain issues?

Are you able and willing to exit your bay?

Do you have the ability and fortitude to help others exit their bays?

Or better yet, as parents especially, are you willing to avoid pure saltwater, and not create bays for your children in the first place?

Luke helped me exit this particular bay in my life. Thank you, Luke.[6]

---

6 To see a picture of Luke and Jenny picking me and Eddie up at the PCT finishline in Canada, go to wewanderpurposefully.com, navigate to the picture menu in the Audiobook section, and click on "Picture 13: Jenny, Eric, Eddie, and Luke"

Chapter 23

Conflict

Much of the contention in the world can be assuaged by looking through parallactic lenses.

By using these lenses, you can disagree civilly with someone you believe is morally wrong. Because people have different upbringings and experiences, conflict is bound to occur.

Conflict is born when two points of view contradict one another. It is the playing out of cognitive dissonance not within one's self, but between two individuals or two groups of individuals.

Contradictory Statement #1: My point of view is right.

Contradictory Statement #2: No, *my* point of view is right.

Since the conflict is not internal, some of the normal ways to counteract cognitive dissonance are ineffective. You cannot diminish the significance of one of the conflicting thoughts because the thoughts are held within two different people. To diminish the importance of one thought is against the will of the one being diminished. You can, however, add new thoughts to the equation through negotiation and compromise (like I do when I over-exercise to compensate for my over-eating). Compromise is an effective action taken to mitigate conflict, but it is a stop-gap measure. Neither side is truly happy, and resentment simmers in the meanwhile.

Many conflicts today look very similar in structure. Most are a variation of the age-old conflict between those who already have something, and those who want that thing.

For example, if you have a bag of French fries, and I'm hungry (pretty much a guarantee), I want you to give me some fries. In fact, seeing as you have so many, I feel it's selfish of you to withhold them.

However, from your point of view, you went to the effort to go get the fries. You have the right to charitably dole out the fries exactly how you see fit. After all, without you, there wouldn't be any fries to begin with.

Under the same logic, if you have a bag of money, and I don't have any money, I want you to give me some money. If you live in America (the land of opportunity), and I am a homeless refugee, I want you to give me American citizenship.

The questions that so often divide us are based upon where to draw the line between selfishness and charity towards potentially undeserving strangers.

The key realization provided by parallax is how both sides of an argument can be perfectly legitimate and reasonable when taken from each side's point of view.

Since we are now looking at these issues in a parallactic way, we now understand that someone may feel differently about an issue because of their unique backgrounds and experiences.

After we admit this reality, we are left with three logical choices to fully resolve our conflicting points of view:

1. Brute Force — The first option is to physically force your adversary to agree with you. This is an often illegal and misdirected enterprise.

2. Persuasion — The second option is to *persuade* your adversary to agree with you. From *Aesop's Fables*:

> A dispute once arose between the Wind and the Sun, which was the stronger of the two, and they agreed to settle the point upon this issue—that whichever of the two soonest made a traveler take off his cloak, should be accounted the more powerful. The Wind began, and blew with all his might and made a blast, cold and fierce as a Thracian storm; but the stronger he blew, the closer the traveler wrapped his cloak around him, and the tighter he grasped it with his hands.
>
> Then broke out the Sun. With his welcome beams he dispersed the vapor and the cold; the traveler felt the genial warmth, and as the Sun shone brighter and brighter, he sat down, quite overcome with the heat, and taking off his cloak, cast it on the ground. Thus the Sun was declared the conqueror; and it has ever been deemed that persuasion is better than force; and that the sunshine of a kind and gentle manner will sooner lay open a poor man's heart

than all the threatenings and force of blustering authority.

Aesop's Fable is sage advice to those enveloped by righteous conflict. If your ultimate goal is to change the viewpoints of a society, and you have no ulterior motives, it is more effective to persuade slowly than to force quickly.

From Martin Luther King Jr.: "Darkness cannot drive out darkness; only light can do that. Hate cannot drive out hate; only love can do that."

3. **Coexistence** — Fortunately, the wisdom of our founding fathers, through freedom of speech and freedom of religion, have built coexistence into the very bones of America. However, social media has made it supremely easy to filter out opposing thought or arguments. You can simply unfriend or unfollow people who think differently than yourself, effectively kicking them out of your consciousness (cue Wilhelm scream).

When you filter out the dissenters, you only see things corresponding with your point of view. Your views are reinforced through repetition, and conflicting ideas are neither presented nor considered.

Today, this is known as an **echo chamber**. An echo chamber is another name for a bay.

Even if you are absolutely convinced you are in the right bay, you need to let different minded people turn your chamber/bay into an estuary.

Some Americans insist their one-sided, perhaps extreme, political views be implemented immediately, through any means necessary. This, no matter what viewpoint you hold, is un-American. Immediate change is unable to happen within the confines of the American Constitution. The freedom of speech endowed by our first amendment forces us to coexist with those who have contrary beliefs. Kathryn Schulz describes the genius of the American Constitution in her book *Being Wrong*:

> We see this in federalism (the sharing of power between national and state governments) and we see it in the system of checks and balances (the sharing of power among legislative, executive, and judicial branches). In both cases, the right to govern is distributed across different entities, to protect against the consolidation of power and ensure that no single viewpoint can drown out the rest. We also see this tolerance for error in the very fact that our laws can be changed; we are free to disagree with our own national past. (This idea, so basic to us that we can't imagine life without it, would have been anathema to most forms of government at most times in history.)

The capacity for peaceful revolution every four years is what keeps our society from imploding upon itself via unending rebellions. Most people don't become violent because they have hope for change in the next election cycle.

All of these competing and entangling forces within our government were created purposely by the Founding Fathers. Some people scream for change NOW, but in so doing, they ironically fail to understand the Constitution. If the Constitution allowed for quick change, the changes they have just quickly implemented could just as quickly be un-implemented.

Until laws change via the democratic process, we need to coexist. It is easier to coexist with people you disagree with if you can learn to see issues from their point of view.

Chapter 24

Pride, Poise, and Courage

The words of Bruce Rollinson, four-time national champion head coach of my football team at Mater Dei High School, are drilled into my brain.

In his trademark raspy bark, he incessantly prioritized three mental virtues of the utmost importance when forming young men and exceptional football players. I will take those mental virtues and apply them, not to football, but to the decisions we have to make on a daily basis.

Virtue 1: <u>PRIDE</u>

Pride entails the belief that who you are, and what you are doing, is the right thing to do. Pride is the driving factor behind our daily decision-making.

It is the opposite of cognitive dissonance. When you are proud, the uncomfortable feelings of cognitive dissonance are not present.

The virtue of pride is sometimes cast in a negative light, and for good reason. The dark side of pride occurs when a person acts without our next virtue: poise.

Virtue 2: POISE

Poise is the glue that keeps society functioning.

To be poised is to roll with the punches when you are unable (perhaps because of cognitive dissonance) to be who your pride dictates you to be, or to do what your pride dictates you should do. Pride might tell you to do something, but a poised person is aware of the negative effects on others his or her pride might incur.

In other words, poise is parallactic, not selfish.

Virtue 3: COURAGE

Courage (whose root word comes from the French word for heart — "*Coeur*") involves taking action to live life according to your pride. You, through pride (the opposite of cognitive dissonance), "know" what is right. I put "know" in quotation marks because your knowing first needs to be dictated by the parallactic features of poise.

As with pride, there is a dark side of courage — occurring as a consequence of the dark side of pride.

You may notice courage and poise are paradoxical. In other words, to act with poise contradicts acting with courage. This is the fine line everyone must walk. There are situations in which one should be poised (purposely *omit* an action), and situations where one should be courageous (purposely commit an action). It is these decisions that make the drama of life worth watching.

The all-too-common, unsettling occurrence of school shootings illustrates the dark side of courage. A school shooter is stuck within his own prideful bay. His senseless act of violence is courageous only within his bay. If he acts only with courage, he will *commit* horrid, pride-induced violence. If he had the mental capacity to act with poise, seeing how his actions would devastate the people around him, he would *omit* those actions.

He is lacking poise, and thinking of nobody but himself. He is thinking of nothing but his own pride.

An example of courage and poise correctly working together would be a working mother who needs to put food on the table for her family. All she wants to do is catch up on sleep, but she instead goes to work so she can afford to feed her children. In this case, the woman is displaying poise *and* courage in her actions. She purposely omits the "selfish" action of sleeping in, and she purposely commits the parallactic action of going to work. Her decision-making (pride) is influenced by poise, and thus leads her towards the correct application of courage.

Of Coach Rollinson's virtues, pride is the easiest. Courage is the hardest. Poise is the most important.

Engaging in Experiential Absorbent Learning is the only action that can help structure your decision-making in situations of cognitive dissonance. Experiential Absorbent Learning has the ability to give you a poised, moral compass to guide your pride. This compass will point you in a direction to empathetically, and thus successfully, base your absorbently and actively gained knowledge.

A person must realize their own, unique perspective is not the only perspective that is real.

A person must realize their own, unique perspective is not the only perspective that *matters*.

The best way to achieve this realization is by engaging in Experiential Absorbent Learning. This can be done by encountering and understanding different cultures, upbringings, and points of view. As I've mentioned before, nowadays it is easier than ever to travel due to advances in transportation. We can put a couple hundred bucks down for a flight and be anywhere within half a day. People can research places to travel to, which restaurants to eat at, where to stay, and what to do while there. Past travel related concerns have been eliminated with readily accessible, impartial review websites (like TripAdvisor and Yelp).

By taking advantage of new travel capabilities, we are more likely to develop parallactic mindsets. We go to new places, experience the kindness of the inhabitants, the beauty of the natural and urban landscapes, and subsequently (and perhaps subconsciously) are more willing to see the world from their point of view.

If you choose not to engage in Experiential Absorbent Learning, be cautious about spewing your opinions on every person and comment section you stumble upon. Rather, listen and read with the intent to learn. Meet people outside of your immediate circle. Realize you don't know what you don't know, and your opinion is just one of billions.

Experiential Absorbent Learning allows you to develop an understanding and empathy for people outside of your comfort zone, community, or bay.

As Aleksandr Solzhenitsyn said in *The Gulag Archipelago*: "What the eyes don't see, the heart doesn't grieve for."

As we End Part 3, here are some takeaway Action Items for Experiential Absorbent Learning:

- Vary your activities.
- Choose activities that challenge you.
- Tell people about your activities to make yourself accountable.
- Travel with the intent to learn, not just to relax.
- Treat people of different perspectives with respect. Understand that those perspectives are the result of unique upbringings and experiences that differ from your own.
- Reserve your right to disagree, but reflect upon the reasons *why* you disagree. Could it be possible you disagree because you are in a bay?
- Act with pride, poise, and courage.
- Follow @etrav_learning on social media and join the Absorbent Learning newsletter for continual inspiration.

Chapter 25

The Stans and You: A Love Song, Return of the Stan

Let's jump back to Visual Absorbent Learning for a sec. Here we have our second meeting with my example, the Stans. Kazakhstan, Kyrgyzstan, Tajikistan, Uzbekistan, Turkmenistan.

Peruse the map and vocalize the names of the countries. Take in their position relative to each other.

At this point, try to see if you can remember all five of the countries' names without looking at the map.

If you want to speed up absorption, it is useful to test yourself for comprehension every once in a while. Testing yourself introduces a psychological phenomenon known as the **Hawthorne Effect**. The Hawthorne Effect occurs when the subjects of an experiment alter their behaviors and performances (effectively devaluing the experiment) because of the extra attention they are getting.

Kids are frequently influenced by the Hawthorne Effect when they are aware of their parents' gaze. They will behave better than if they were not being monitored because of the potential consequences of bad behavior.

Testing yourself is a self-induced Hawthorne Effect. If you are testing yourself, and keeping tabs on how much progress you are or are not making, you will study more often. You will absorb faster.

If you find yourself struggling to remember, here are a few memory techniques borrowed from the world of active learning:

1. **Gain some context.** When trying to remember the names of foreign words, it can sometimes be helpful to familiarize yourself with the word's etymology.

   For example, let's break down the word "Kazakhstan" into its parts. Upon cursory research, it turns out that the word "Kazakh" is derived from the Turkic word "Qaz" which means "to wander." Fun fact: this also happens to be the same root word for Cossack, the historically fierce Russian warrior wanderers.

   Moving along, the Persian suffix "stan" literally means "the place of", completing Kazakhstan's meaning as, "The place of the wanderers." Knowing the word's background can make memorization experiences more entertaining than rote memorization. Your brain becomes more invested, and thus more interested in remembering the information.

Kazakh Purposefully!

2. **Take the easy wins**. The biggest country, bigger than the other 4 combined, is Kazakhstan. You might also realize that Kazakh's relation to Cossack makes it most likely to be the one Stan that borders Russia. That should make it easier to remember.

   Turkmenistan (literally meaning "the place of the Turk men") is the closest Stan to the country of Turkey. If you know where Turkey is, this should make Turkmenistan's position relatively easy to remember.

3. **Look for patterns**. These patterns could be in a geographic sense or in a morphological (study of the structure of words) sense. Kazakhstan and Kyrgyzstan border each other and both start with the letter K. Turkmenistan and Tajikistan are the southernmost and both start with T. Uzbekistan is in the middle and the only one that doesn't start with K or T.

4. **Make a mnemonic device**. Moving clockwise starting with Kazakhstan, the Stans are as follows: Kazakhstan, Kyrgyzstan, Tajikistan, Uzbekistan, and Turkmenistan. Now, create a mnemonic device by taking the first letter of each country. This leaves us with KKTUT.

   I'll always remember Kazakhstan because it was our easy win so I can shorten the mnemonic to KTUT. An easy way for me to remember KTUT is to associate it with the famous Egyptian pharaoh Tutankhamun, colloquially known as King Tut. When we recall that Turkmenistan is the closest Stan to Turkey, we can easily differentiate which T is Turkmenistan and which T is Tajikistan.

PART 4

Absorbent Learning as a Lifestyle

Chapter 26

Linear Learning

"My fellow nerds and I will retire to the nerdery with our calculators."
— DAVID SPADE, TOMMY BOY

The three types of Absorbent Learning supplement each other, and you can practice them in any order you'd like.

At the start of this book, I told you how my mother placing the periodic table in my "white space" had cascading influences throughout my life: her action was the first of many linearly connected curiosities. Each curiosity added more color to the ones that came after it. Ultimately, the periodic table tacked above my bed kickstarted my cascading learning process. I am very aware of the folly of crediting correlation with causation, but I also recognize the linear momentum gathered by a single event.

If you travel to Italy, you're more likely to travel to Greece, and then travel to Albania.

If you read *The Iliad*, you're more likely to read *The Odyssey*, and then read *The Aeneid*.

If you learn who the 1st Roman Emperor was, you're more likely to learn the 2nd and 3rd.

The more you uncover gaps in your knowledge, the more knowledge you gain.

From listening to Mary Beard's *SPQR* while hiking on the windy ridges of the Goat Rocks Wilderness in southern Washington on the PCT[1], I learned about Roman history from 796 BC until 212 AD. I know a lot about ancient Rome now, but also know nothing about the Roman empire from 212 AD until its eventual dissolution in 1453 AD. I'm aware of a gap in my knowledge, and am now more likely to seek answers to fill that gap.

This is known in behavioral economics as the Gap Theory. The first step to a desire for knowledge is to pinpoint a lack of knowledge. I've become more interested in history in general because I know about ancient Rome.

Additionally, I use Visual Absorbent Learning to support Auditory Absorbent Learning by saving my favorite quotations/ideas, and posting them in a white space. This way I won't forget what I've listened to. If you are willing and able to do this too, you will notice how it influences your subsequent actions.

Your Visual Absorbent Learning can also supplement your Experiential Absorbent Learning. You may travel to countries you otherwise wouldn't have if you prime yourself by studying geography.

---

1 To see a picture of me packing up camp in the Goat Rocks Wilderness with Mount Rainier in the background, go to wewanderpurposefully.com, navigate to the picture menu in the Audiobook section, and click on "Picture 14: Mount Rainier"

Nerdery encourages more nerdery. Nerdery always has been a good thing, but nowadays it holds more social clout. Nerds are cool.

Even football, a sport dominated by jocks, is increasingly becoming more and more nerdy with the explosion of statistical analysis. The league hires experts whose sole job is to pinpoint which particular plays and actions are more statistically likely to result in concussions. Scouts put a particular emphasis on things like ankle flexion and arm length when measuring college prospects. If you are an offensive lineman and your arms aren't at least 33 inches long, you'll likely be a guard or a center instead of a tackle (as a side note, tackles get paid much more on average than guards or centers — a finding that can be chalked up as an arm length tax).

NFL teams are also increasingly paying big bucks for a service called Pro Football Focus. It takes after baseball's "Moneyball" sabermetrics, and is football nerdery at its finest. Pro Football Focus supplies coaches with esoteric data, like what percentage of overall plays the quarterback performed a pump fake, or the exact hang time of punts and kickoffs (to two decimal places).

It's time to fully embrace your inner nerd. You'll be attuning yourself to all the other closet nerds out there.

Chapter 27

The Secret Password

"You're my favorite deputy!"
— **WOODY**, TOY STORY

I repeat: Absorbent Learning helps you create weak ties faster and easier.

When you relate with someone using the knowledge you've gained from Absorbent Learning, you are showcasing a genuine desire to connect with them. This desire to connect will likely be reciprocated. You have made a personable first move to establish a connection, thus encouraging your new connection to let their guard down.

Back in the Introduction, I mentioned how saying "thank you" to my Ethiopian Uber driver in his native language was an example of attunement. This sort of attunement is *always* positive.

What we are doing here is exploiting a heuristic known in psychology as the **Halo Effect**. Daniel Kahneman gives another example of the Halo Effect in *Thinking, Fast and Slow*. He explains a hypothetical situation wherein you meet a woman named Joan at a party and find her to be a delightful conversationalist. After meeting her, you are asked whether or not Joan would be likely to contribute to a charity. What do we know about Joan? Kahneman writes:

> You know virtually nothing, because there is little reason to believe that people who are agreeable in social situations are also generous contributors to charities.
>
> But you like Joan and you will retrieve the feeling of liking her when you think of her. You also like generosity and generous people… you are now predisposed to believe…Joan is generous. And now that you believe she is generous, you probably like Joan even better than you did earlier, because you have added generosity to her pleasant attributes.

We don't actually have any reason to think Joan is generous, but we do anyways because of our heuristic Halo response to her character.

Think of the Halo Effect as being the opposite of wearing a New England Patriots hat outside of New England. Everybody dislikes, or at least are jealous of the Patriots because of their sustained NFL success over decades. At some point, your team has suffered defeat versus the Patriots. Subsequently, you have an inherent heuristic dislike for all things Patriot. If you see someone with a Patriot hat on, you preternaturally dislike that person without knowing anything else about them. They have created a negative Halo Effect (a devil horns effect?) as a first impression. If you are a Patriot fan, take off that hat!

When attunement occurs, even only superficially, we are on the first steps toward this harmony becoming a norm of society. Norms, or shared communal expectations on what is appropriate, come in several different forms. For the rest of this chapter, we will discuss what happens when a community acts via **social norms** instead of **market norms**.

Market norms occur, for example, when you walk into a shop, pay a specified amount of money for a good or service, and then receive said good or service in return. The course of events is predictable, and the value of goods has been established. There's rarely any meaningful or memorable interactions when we act according to market norms.

However, when attunement is the focal point of a relationship, we start to act more in accordance with social norms than market norms.

On the PCT, there is a common phenomenon known as "trail magic." Trail magic illustrates what I mean by social norms. You will be having a rough day after hiking miles and miles, and suddenly a complete stranger does something kind for you. Trail magic can come in the form of a ride into a town, a free place to stay, or sometimes even a trailside buffet of free beers, sodas, gatorades, fruit, sandwiches, brats, burgers, and friendship.

Trail magic exists because of attunement.

Almost without fail, the stranger is a past hiker who has experienced trail magic themselves, and is now paying it forward. They know exactly what it's like to be a thru-hiker, and what a joy it is to receive a hot meal or a cold drink. Believe me when I say there is nothing else in the world a hiker would rather have except maybe a shower.

In this interaction, the good or service is kindness, and the currency is paying this kindness forward when it's my time to provide trail magic to future hikers.

What results is a communal fellowship based not upon money, but upon friendship and goodwill.

I'm not advocating for a society based only on social norms. In capitalism, we need market norms to establish the objective value of goods and to sustain a free marketplace.

What I *am* advocating for is a thawing of the icy demeanor I so often witness amongst strangers (this is commonly known in Seattle as the Seattle Freeze). If we were more attuned to those around us, social norms would replace market norms, and grease the wheels of friendship amongst people. Imagine a world where to buy a stranger a drink was simply a gesture of friendship, instead of an instance of blatant flirtation or brownnosing.

That is the world I want to live in, and, fortunately, it exists within certain communities. The thru-hiking, rugby, and après-ski communities are prime examples. The shared interest in a preferred activity supplies the attunement necessary for social norms to prevail.

These three communities I've just mentioned have their own separate customs and lingoes, indecipherable to those unattuned to their respective activity.

A thru-hiker is familiar with terms like guthook, nero, and nobo. They also have their own "secret" handshake only other hikers are privy to (it's just a simple fist-bump). Thru-hikers even eschew their given first name and surname, and replace it with what is known as a "trail-name" while ontrail. I was dubbed "Eric the Red" on the second day of the trail because I was getting annoying nosebleeds. I shortened the nickname to "Red" because the real Viking Erik the Red spelled his name with a "k" and I'm an anti Eric-with-a-k guy.

Ruggers also have terms with unique meanings like maul, ruck, line-out, and scrum. They also sing participatory songs during after-match socials in which BOTH opposing teams come together to celebrate the sport of rugby.

Après skiers (après literally means "after" in French) drink, dance, and party in 70s style outfits, with their ski boots on, and you might hear them say: "The pow from Spanky's Ladder to Catskinner to Lower Gear Jammer was awesome today!"

Uncoincidentally, my favorite part of these activities is not the activity itself, but the attunement I experience with others while taking part in them — meeting other hikers (not hiking itself), after-match socials (not rugby itself), and the "après" part of skiing (not skiing itself).

Lingoes and customs act like secret passwords for inclusion in these communities.

If you can demonstrate your thru-hiker-ness by introducing yourself with your trail name and a hiker handshake, you have supplied the secret password, signalled your attunement, and gained a new weak tie within 5 seconds. Your race, gender, sexuality, religion, political leanings, along with everything else, do not matter. The entrenched, destructive, societal archetypes of homophily have been overthrown. That's how the thru-hiking community works. It is beautiful. And it's because social norms have replaced market norms.

All you need to benefit from the social norms of certain communities is the secret password of attunement provided by that community's lingo and customs.

That is exactly what the Absorbent Learning lifestyle provides.

Chapter 28

The Ancestral Telephone

Religions are quintessential examples of exclusive communities ruled by specific lingoes and customs. A religion is essentially a lifestyle in itself. People spend time attending religious events, but faith is often a much larger part of their lives than those few hours spent in a place of worship. Religion regularly influences a person's daily decision-making because there are normally clear external incentives. For example, if someone is Christian, they are less likely to murder someone because it is expressly forbidden within their Judeo-Christian beliefs. On top of the legal ramifications, there is the threat of eternal damnation if they commit wanton murder.

Karl Marx famously pronounced: "Religion is the opiate of the masses." Many cite his quotation when bashing the existence of religion, likening it to a harmful drug. My intention is not to bash religion. Rather, I put forth Marx's quotation to focus on a single word: masses. Many *many* people identify themselves as religious, and *all* people can act as gateway opportunities in life as weak ties.

According to a survey conducted by the Pew Research Center in 2015, if you are Christian, a whopping 68.8% of the world believes differently than you do, of which only 16% of the world's population identify themselves as unaffiliated with any religion at all.

That means, regardless of which religion you belong to, at least 52.8% of the world actively practices an entirely different religion than you do.

I spent much of my scholastic life in Catholic institutions, yet barely so much as cracked *The Bible* open outside of religion classes. As a result, I had knowledge of a decent amount of passages in the New Testament, but only those that had been drilled into my brain. Even so, as I began the PCT, I had a deep-seated feeling that if I were to identify myself as a Christian, it would be hypocritical of me to not have taken the time to read the Holy Book of the religion I was claiming to be.

Cognitive dissonance alert:

Contradictory Statement #1: I am Catholic.
Contradictory Statement #2: I haven't read *The Bible*.

I listened to the New Testament (rectifying Statement #2) while trekking through the Sonoran and Mojave deserts (coincidentally spending 40+ days there), and I felt immediately better.[2] I was no longer a walking cognitive dissonant in that regard. After finishing it, I needed another book to fill my end-

---

2   To see a picture of me setting off into the Mojave Desert, go to wewanderpurposefully.com, navigate to the picture menu in the Audiobook section, and click on "Picture 15: Mojave Desert".

of-day trail listening. It was then when it occurred to me I could listen to other Holy Books as well.

I questioned: "If I read the New Testament, why wouldn't I read the Old Testament, or the Quran, or any other religion's Holy Book?"

The first reason that came to mind was obvious: "I was raised a Catholic, and nothing else." Chiding myself, I was reminded of an Aristotle quote I listened to during the first few weeks of the trail in Mark Manson's *The Subtle Art of Not Giving a *****: "It is the mark of an educated mind to be able to entertain a thought without accepting it." When thinking in this Aristotelian manner, my averseness to another religion's Holy Book seemed petty and closed-minded.

Once in that mindset, my only remaining excuse seemed to be: I simply didn't care about other people's religions. When equating religions and lifestyles, it could then be said as an extension that I didn't care about other people in general.

That was an answer that didn't sit well with me. After experiencing trail magic, as well as kindness in my past travels from people of all different religions, I realized I was being inconsistent with my real feelings. Again, I was struck with the uncomfortableness provided by cognitive dissonance.

Religion is, after all, like many other identifiers, essentially a reflection of one's upbringing. William James in *The Will to Believe* famously opined: "Our faith is faith in someone else's faith and in the greatest matters this is most the case."

Indeed, the greatest determinant of a person's religious leanings are the religious leanings of their parents. This begs the question: "Why are *my* parents any more correct than someone else's parents?" This question, ultimately unanswerable if considered without bias, begs another question: "Where did my parents get their beliefs?" The answer to this question is almost invariably from their own parents, whose beliefs were influenced by *their* parents, and so on through the generations until you reach the conversion of some distant ancestor via force or happenstance.

Oftentimes, this distant conversion event is completely shrouded by the passage of time and unsupported by video or photographic evidence. The evidence we do have is in real danger of being taken out of context, or distorted through generations of oral tradition.

This distortion can be compared to the children's game of Telephone. When playing Telephone, children stand in a circle wherein the game's originator whispers a sentence into the ear of the next child in the circle. That next child then repeats what they think they heard to the *next* child in the circle. Once the sentence has traveled the entire circle and been relayed back to the original whisperer, it usually no longer remotely resembles what was originally said.

Now multiply the telephonic nature of oral tradition with the instability (revolutions, plagues, Inquisitions, crusades, etc.) and biases (women's rights, racism, homophobia, bloodletting, etc.) that pockmark distant time periods. All evidence is put in question to some degree.

Without any credible evidence, who am I to judge whether my own ancestor's conversion is more or less authentic than somebody else's ancestor? And, as an extension, why then, in the 21st century, should I form judgment on someone else based on their religion?

In *The Divine Comedy*, Dante Alighieri presents a profound hypothetical:

> A man is born on the banks of the Indus, and no one is there who may speak of Christ, nor who may read, nor who may write; and all his wishes and acts are good so far as human reason sees, without sin in life or in speech. He dies unbaptized, and without faith: where is this justice which condemns him? Where is his sin if he does not believe?

Had I been born in a Muslim country, with Muslim parents, I would no doubt be Muslim. Whether a person believes in God, Jehovah, Allah, any other deity, or nothing at all, they have only been playing a different game of Ancestral Telephone.

Therefore, disrespecting someone else's religion is essentially tantamount to disrespecting their parents and ancestry as well. As can be witnessed in many of the world's scuffles, dissing a person's mother or father outright can be an unfortunately explosive affair.

I have too much respect for my own parents and ancestors to abandon the Catholic Church. To do so, no matter how many dogmatical doubts I might entertain, would be a slap in the face of my upbringing. My upbringing made me who I am today, and I cannot, in good conscience, deny the part the Catholic Church has played in my formation.

Cognitive dissonance (simultaneous contradictory belief and behavior) does not rule the day in this case. My belief is not solely rooted in the religion itself, but also in my family tradition. My behavior is to continue that tradition. I will respect my Ancestral Telephone.

I encourage you to respect your own Ancestral Telephone while simultaneously respecting everyone else's Ancestral Telephone. I'm not telling you to become an all-knowing authority on all of these religions. I listened to *The Bible*, *The Holy Quran*, *The Book of Mormon*, and *The Analects of Confucius* during the PCT, but notice how I haven't quoted any of those Holy Books in this chapter. I don't pretend to be a Quran scholar. I listened to it only once, and can't quote a single word. Pretending I am a fount of Quranic wisdom would be affectatious and pretentious. Nevertheless, I *have* listened to it, and I therefore am more attuned to every Muslim I come across. **I have created superficial knowledge where before there was *zero* knowledge.**

In my personal experience, many people's outward knowledge of Islam consists of the 9/11 terror attacks coupled with *Team America: World Police* jokes.

If people took some of their white space to listen to the Quran, they'd be able to say "I've read the Quran." This would be a manifest show of respect, an admirable action.

A majority of the world bases their lifestyle on different religious books. Yet most of us don't care enough to take the time to read them. I often see loud people get on soap boxes to say how they don't judge people based on their religions. Anyone can say that. They can even mean it. But they haven't put the time in to justify that statement. It's like a person telling you they support you as a writer when they haven't taken the time to read your book. It's disingenuous and see-through. I say, prove it! Put your time where your mouth is, and read the Holy Books of other cultures. If you utilize the white space in your day, you don't have the time/motivation excuse. The only excuse you have for not doing it is because you don't care enough about other people to do it.

I repeat: respect your own Ancestral Telephone while also respecting everyone else's Ancestral Telephone. To quote Shakespeare's *Hamlet*: "There are more things in heaven and earth, Horatio, than are dreamt of in our philosophy." Respect other people's Telephones, and those people will respect you *as a person*. If you are Christian, you would be following the Golden Rule anyways: treat others as you would like to be treated. It's a Win win!

Assuredly I say to you that the mere action of taking the time (time that was in your white spaces anyways) to respect a person's lifestyle, especially when it is not realistically expected of you to do so, speaks for itself. It is more authentic than any pandering words could ever be. The superficiality of your knowledge does not ring hollow because so few people expend the extreme effort you have. You are unique.

Read the Holy Books, and you'll not only cure cognitive dissonance, but you'll also start to notice the relational advantages you now have when you come across someone of a different religion.

As my own example, a surprising amount of fervent Israeli Jews were hiking the PCT, fresh off of their nationally required military service. When their faith popped up in conversation, I would drop a quick "I just read the Torah" comment. This was a quick attunement. Suddenly, they would look at me with new eyes, surprised that someone, especially a Gentile, would take the time to respect their lifestyle in such an extreme way.

The Torah is part of the Old Testament. The Old Testament is 57 hours long on audiobook, and most of it is unbelievably dry reading in dire need of a good editor (shoutout to the book of Chronicles). However, because I listened to it, there's a much greater chance Jewish people will experience a Halo Effect when talking to me. What's more, because this interaction was my first interaction with them, I will experience another boost by making a good first impression. In doing so, I am making a stronger connection with these strangers by taking advantage of their natural biases and heuristics.

Absorbent Learning is a lifestyle. It's a way of thinking and living; therefore, you might even call it a religion by extension. Absorbent Learning allows you to respect your own Ancestral Telephone while also respecting everyone else's Ancestral Telephones.

Where most religions require you to actively spend time praying to a specific deity, Absorbent Learning invites you to spend your *white space time* learning about everyone else's deities.

Chapter 29

Taking Flight

"We are what we repeatedly do. Excellence, then, is not an act, but a habit."

— **WILL DURANT**, THE STORY OF PHILOSOPHY

Cultivating a love for learning is no different than cultivating any other habit. Habits are only cemented into our daily routine through practice. Practice has the power to literally change our brains. How exactly does practice achieve this feat? In *The Happiness Advantage*, Harvard PhD Shawn Achor describes how repeated experience and practice literally reconfigures the brain's structure:

> Within our brains are billions upon billions of neurons, interconnect-

ed in every which way to form a complex set of neural pathways. Electrical currents travel down these pathways, from neuron to neuron, delivering the messages that make up our every thought and action. The more we perform a particular action, the more connections form between the corresponding neurons... The stronger this link, the faster the message can travel down the pathway. This is what makes the behavior seem second nature, or automatic.

Remember how I got better at listening to audiobooks as I progressed along the PCT? This happened because I had made a habit of listening. My brain had created an entrenched network of neural pathways through practice.

So how do we motivate ourselves to practice and create new habits? A month after the PCT I listened to a luminary book called *The Power of Habit* by Charles Duhigg. One of Duhigg's main ideas is how easy it is to create good habits (or destroy bad habits), once you know how a habit is structured. In his book, he breaks down the structure of habits into what is called the "habit loop." There are three parts of the habit loop: the **cue**, the **routine**, and the **reward**.

Think of the cue-routine-reward habit loop as the procedure we perform when training dogs, falcons, or infants. The cue is the action we perform to signal the dog. For example, when we point to the ground and yell "Sit!" The routine is the dog performing the desired sitting action. The reward is the treat given to the dog after successful performance of the command. We are basically creating new Pavlovian habits for the dog based upon their instinctual cravings for treats.

So how can we make Absorbent Learning a habit for ourselves? Well, taking what we've learned from Duhigg, you need a cue, a routine, and a reward.

Let's take my personal Visual Absorbent Learning technique as an example. The cue and the routine are easy. My cue is the act of stepping into the shower every morning and seeing my world map. The routine is my action of mentally studying my world map while physically performing my showerly hygiene procedure.

The tricky part of the Absorbent Learning habit loop is the reward. The reward isn't concrete like a dog treat. External incentives, like trophies or passing grades on tests, don't exist for Absorbent Learning. This is the main reason why people may not think Absorbent Learning is worthwhile. The main criticism for Absorbent Learning is the perceived triviality of the subjects being learned. I hope, by now, that I have convinced you of just how un-trivial the rewards of Absorbent Learning can be.

Even when a person receives a reward from Absorbent Learning, they normally don't recognize Absorbent Learning as their mysterious benefactor. Say you bond with a person by flawlessly rapping the lyrics to a song you've listened to on repeat during your commute. You might not consciously credit your Absorbent Learning technique for this small victory, but it nonetheless is the action that deserves credit. That person is impressed by your rapping skillz. At this point you've experienced the reward portion of the cue-routine-reward habit loop of Absorbent Learning.

Absorbent learning is like a boarding gate at an airport, and new relationships, careers, and ideas are the flights. There are thousands of flights, but you can't take off without first being at the correct boarding gate number.

Being at the correct boarding gate is *ultra important* before getting on a flight. But after takeoff you likely don't remember your boarding gate number, nor do you celebrate the fact that that boarding gate was responsible for your successful boarding. Likewise, when you disembark at your final destination, you probably do not notice which boarding gate you walk through upon exiting the plane.

Sometimes we do not give credit where credit is due. Absorbent Learning, like your boarding gate, is often behind the inception of your new relationships and ideas.

Make a habit of celebrating your boarding gate.

A new habit starts with one new action. Mother Teresa made a habit of helping those desperately in need on the streets of Calcutta: "Maybe if I didn't pick up that one person, I wouldn't have picked up forty-two thousand... the same thing goes for you, the same thing in your family, the same thing in your church, your community. Just begin — one, one, one."

One fact learned. It could be the capital of Mexico (Mexico City!).

One book listened to. Maybe some Doctor Seuss.

One place traveled to. Maybe start with the restaurant across town. It doesn't have to be a mountain summit.[3]

Upon repetition, your habit becomes easier to perform. If you perform a habit enough times, you'll start seeing that habit in the world around you.

There is a psychological phenomenon known as the **Tetris Effect** that accounts for this sentiment. I first heard about the Tetris Effect on-trail while listening to Shawn Achor's *The Happiness Advantage*. Harvard Medical School researchers coerced test subjects to play Tetris for multiple hours on end for three days straight, and then studied the after effects. Test subjects went on record saying they were seeing Tetris blocks everywhere they went, even falling out of the sky.

The researchers explained these temporary delusions were the result of what they termed a "cognitive afterimage." These afterimages were akin to the blue and green blind spots we commonly experience after a camera flashes

---

[3] To see a picture of Eddie and me on the summit of Mount Whitney, go to wewanderpurposefully.com, navigate to the picture menu in the Audiobook section, and click on "Picture 16: Mount Whitney"

directly into our eyes. The excessive gameplay had created brand new neural pathways, or cognitive afterimages, within the brain.

I experience the Tetris Effect when it comes to learning. This is what I've been referring to all along as my "love for learning." Honestly, it *is* a little insane. From my sheer amount of Absorbent Learning, I've become obsessed with it. I can't stop my mind from being habitually curious. I see the things around me, and I'm immediately curious as to what I can possibly learn from them.

I'm overwhelmingly attracted to the idea of pursuing knowledge. I'm so attracted to it that I rationalized walking a ludicrous amount of miles, mainly because I realized walking all day granted me white space for an invaluable learning opportunity.

By making a habit of Absorbent Learning, you will also experience the Tetris effect and notice the countless learning opportunities surrounding your life.

Everybody has their own obsessions; a learning obsession is one of the most positive obsessions a person can have.

Chapter 30

The Virtuous Circle

"You can't inject someone with education the way you can with a vaccine. You can't force it upon people. They have to reach out and work for it themselves."

— **ADAM BRAUN**, THE PROMISE OF A PENCIL

People can do anything they put their minds to if they are sufficiently motivated.

Sometimes, our motivation comes in the form of bribery, disguised as salary. Other times, our motivation is simply self-preservation. It is, however, the illogical things we do for the mere satisfaction of doing them that provides evidence of an intrinsically powerful motivator. We call this motivator **love**.

The power of love is evident in all areas of life, but this chapter is about school specifically. The fact is, most kids don't like school. They go to class grudgingly, sometimes kicking and screaming. The worst part is, I can't blame them. I didn't like school very much, and I was actually really good at it.

The external incentive to do well in high school is the allure of inclusion in exclusive clubs. These clubs have names like Harvard College and the Dean's List. Put aside the fabricated prestige of belonging to these clubs, and let's take a closer look at what it means to "do well" in school today.

What does doing well in school entail? It is based mainly on objective measures, namely grade point average and SAT/ACT test scores. The problem with this type of testing is that there is a direct correlation between how successful you are on the test, and how well you prepare for that *specific* test.

To illustrate this point, I'll use the Mechanical Fundamentals of Engineering Exam, which my classmates and I were required to take after completing our undergraduate engineering degrees. This exam, known simply as the FE, is intended for students who have finished the full four year course-load of mechanical engineering. Because I chose not to major in mechanical engineering, but rather to major in Engineering Management (of which there is no specific Fundamentals of Engineering Exam), I took classes on two-thirds of the material covered on the FE.

The FE test has about a 78% pass rate amongst its candidates, and you have to pay a few hundred bucks to take the test (so nobody is taking it for fun). For some context, the Bar Exam, taken to become a licensed attorney in the United States, has an approximate 75% pass rate amongst first-time takers. Granted, people study much longer for the Bar Exam because of the sheer amount of rote memorization and essay skills required to pass it.

Basically, I was taking an engineering test that 1 in 5 people fail after four years of the required course load. I was at a severe disadvantage because I took only about two and a half years of the course load, with the rest of my course load being business classes.

My preparation for the FE consisted of one week of studying. First, I purchased and completed one practice FE test to establish a baseline for my knowledge. I got a demoralizing 23% on it. After completion of the practice test, I was granted access to a solutions manual providing the steps I *should* have taken to solve every problem correctly. I then combed through every solution to every problem, and learned the procedure for solving that *specific type* of problem. I took the FE one week later, and passed.

Passing the FE means I can put the Engineer-in-Training (EIT) designation on my resume. It also provides me the opportunity to become a Professional Engineer (PE) in the future by passing the PE test.

But what does passing this test *really* mean for my education? I actively crammed procedures into my brain for one week. After I passed, I immediately forgot all of those procedures because there was no longer an external incentive for me to remember them.

All passing the FE Exam shows is I've mastered how to pass that *particular* test.

As many graduates trying to get jobs out of college can attest, there is a wide gulf of usefulness between school skills, practical skills, and skills you learn on the job. Job skills and practical skills are learned via *experience*, not school. I have become a wizard at passing engineering tests, but that does not translate or become useful when I venture outside the confines of theoretical word problems.

You can go through high school and college, pass every test, earn degrees, and *still* feel like you've retained almost nothing beyond friendships, vocabulary, and critical thinking skills. This is a poor reflection on the incentive structure of college itself. This structure takes those who love learning, forces them to temporarily memorize things, and thus makes them dread going to class.

There are a few deeper things that happen when our biggest incentive in school is, not to learn, but to do well on tests for the purpose of admittance to exclusive clubs. Because everyone is primed to strive for the exclusive clubs, the few that actually become part of them have a superiority complex (even if they manage to hide it well) over everyone who did not. What happens to the overwhelming majority of kids who don't make it into the most exclusive clubs? Our omnipresent frenemy, cognitive dissonance, happens:

Contradictory Statement #1: I want to belong to the most exclusive clubs.
Contradictory Statement #2: I did not make the cut for the exclusive clubs.

Remember, there are a few ways to deal with cognitive dissonance. Two such ways are to diminish the significance of one of the conflicting thoughts, or to add a third compensating thought to the equation. How students deal with this type of cognitive dissonance is ultra-important. It may be in one (or a combination) of the following four ways:

1. The healthiest way is to diminish the significance of the first thought "I want to belong to the most exclusive clubs" by saying to yourself: "Belonging to the exclusive club is not important."

    We are lucky if any student says this because they have been primed by their parents, classmates, and the education system itself to believe admittance into these clubs *is* important.

2. The second, not as healthy way, is to add the following thought to the battle: "At least I made it into another club, even if it's not as exclusive as the club I was hoping for."

    This thought occurs when you don't make the cut for a prestigious college like Harvard, but do make the cut for a less prestigious college.

There are a couple of underlying issues here:
Firstly, you still hold a superiority complex over those who settled for schools even less prestigious than yours. At this point, you're no better, and even more petty, than the Harvardians. Secondly, you still hold the "I want to belong to the most exclusive clubs" thought in your mind, and it may eat away at you for the rest of your life. Or, if you let it, it could give you a spiteful, yet productive, chip on your shoulder.

3. The third, perhaps unhealthiest, way is to add the thought: "It's not fair."

Although I agree it isn't fair, this sort of thought is a big contributor to the helpless victim mentality that plagues our country. People are blaming everybody but themselves. White people blame affirmative action. Minorities blame white people. Poor people blame rich people. Women blame the patriarchy. Men blame Title IX. Everybody starts getting *angry* at anything and everything that had to do with their own inability to make the cut. Anger is not the most productive of emotions. Anger leads to hate, and hate leads to tragedy.

4. The very least healthy way is to add the thought: "I'm not smart enough."

Unfortunately, some people do not do well in school. School is not everyone's "thing." Moreover, there are mental disabilities and extenuating circumstances like issues at home that cause kids to slip through the cracks. Many students are left feeling like failures. However, as Albert Einstein said: "Everybody is a genius. But if you judge a fish by its ability to climb a tree, it will live its whole life believing that it is stupid."

The second, third and fourth ways to deal with this type of cognitive dissonance are extremely unhealthy.

Society is sick.

Society is sick because of the steady diet of exclusivity we feed our children, starting from day zero. We are teaching our kids to place the highest value on accomplishments that look good from the outside.

Because it is difficult to visualize the amorphous concept of learning, it would be helpful to draw a visual analogy to illustrate how misguided the school incentive system is. To do this, we will think of the differences between Mr. Universe competition participants (also known as bodybuilders) and the World's Strongest Man Competition participants (also known as strongmen).

We know bodybuilders as the oiled-up Adonises strutting their stuff up on the Mr. Universe stage. The Mr. Universe contest requires athletes to stand in a myriad of poses while judges score them on the size and pleasing outward aesthetic of their muscles. Thus, incentivized by the rules of Mr. Universe, bodybuilders focus on building glamour muscles through isolation exercises (exercises that stress a single muscle group) like bicep curls or tricep extensions.

In contrast, we know strongmen as the behemoths flipping cars, tossing kegs, and heaving enormous boulders in the World's Strongest Man contest. To be World's Strongest Man, one must outlift and outpersevere the other competing athletes. Unlike bodybuilders, strongmen do not particularly care about glamour muscles: they focus on building overall strength via compound exercises (exercises that stress *multiple* muscle groups) such as power cleans, deadlifts, and squats.

These are two different styles of athletes, with two different training regimens, based on two differing incentives. Their different regimens lead to different body types. Strongmen look less like 1970's Arnold Schwarzenegger, and more like sentient tree trunks.

Both of these types of athletes spend their waking hours working on their physiques, but which would you rather have help you if you were trapped under a burning car?

As it turns out, strongmen are objectively stronger than their bodybuilding counterparts in almost every measurable strength category. This is because of the emphasis put upon developing *all* of their muscles, instead of only their glamour muscles.

The current education system is equivalent to the Mr. Universe pageant: our mental reps are building towards glamourous external incentives. When we are cramming for specific tests to gain admittance to exclusive clubs, we are repping isolation exercises. Our degrees and test scores make us look good on the outside. But that doesn't make us smart.

If our active learning education system would incentivize long-term learning, it would become more like the World's Strongest Man competition. We would be repping compound exercises. Intelligence would be more valuable than glamour.

Learning journeys like my PCT PhD would be just as celebrated as traditional PhD's.

Which education system would you rather have determining our world's future? A glamourous one or an effective one?

I'm not advocating kids do away with today's education. That's how things are done successfully in a capitalistic society.

What I *am* advocating for is twofold:

1. We, as parents, should not be blind to the shallowness we are teaching our children. When our ultimate goal is for our children to be part of an exclusive club (non-coincidentally, making ourselves seem like better parents in the process), we are teaching them that being in an exclusive club is the only thing they should strive for. Along the way, they will eschew less important goals. Like actually maintaining the information learned in their classes.

2. We, as voters in a democratic society, should change the education system to somehow incentivize learning over test scores. I've pinpointed the problem, but don't yet have a full, quantifiable solution. I'm hopeful one of you will find one.

So how can we encourage kids to wade through the misguided incentives of the American school system, while also teaching them the importance of learning for the sake of learning?

How can we teach them that learning things is more important than being in exclusive clubs?

How can we encourage them to love learning?

Even though I don't have a full solution to the problem, I do have a partial one. You guessed it. My partial solution is Absorbent Learning.

Absorbent Learning doesn't eliminate the exclusive club incentive, but it *can* motivate kids to love learning.

To illustrate my proposed partial solution, I want to share the following from Malcolm Gladwell. In *Outliers*, Gladwell discusses the objective statistical test score superiority of Chinese children versus Western children in the subject of mathematics, as researched by Karen Fuson at Northwestern University. Fuson believes the faster, more intuitive, way numbers translate in Chinese as opposed to English, plays a significant role in the success Chinese children have in mathematics:

> For fractions we say three-fifths. The Chinese translation is literally, "out of five parts, take three." That's telling you conceptually what a fraction is. It's differentiating the denominator and the numerator. The much-storied disenchantment with mathematics among Western children starts in the third and fourth grade, and Fuson argues that perhaps a part of that disenchantment is due to the fact that math doesn't seem to make sense; its linguistic structure is clumsy; its basic rules seem arbitrary and complicated.
>
> Asian children, by contrast, don't face nearly that same sense of bafflement. They can hold more numbers in their head, and do calculations faster, and the way fractions are expressed in their language corresponds exactly to the way a fraction actually is — and maybe that makes them a little more likely to enjoy math, and maybe because they enjoy math a little more they try a little harder and take more math classes and are more willing to do their homework, and on and on, in a kind of virtuous circle.

Gladwell's virtuous circle is the embodiment of what I want *Wander Purposefully* to accomplish. If we can show students that knowing things, even if they seem trivial, is its own incentive, then they will enter a virtuous circle. They will *want* to learn.

Let's say a child has just graduated from the third grade and is now on summer vacation. Then, you, as a parent, place a visual learning device in the child's white space introducing them to their upcoming fourth grade curriculum. This would prime the child for their fourth grade subjects, and give him/her a leg up on understanding various subjects once the school year rolls around.

In turn, the child is now more confident, more participatory, and more interested during class.

The dopamine-laced act of knowing the answer when a question is asked is pleasurable (ask any *Jeopardy*! fanatic or trivia game participant). Kids will be *addicted* to knowing things, and will thus seek knowledge willingly.

Take a closer look at addiction, AKA doing illogical things for the sake of doing them, and you will notice it isn't a whole lot different than love.

Visual Absorbent Learning is like making flash cards for a test, but never throwing them away because there aren't any scheduled tests. The tests pop up organically throughout your life within your conversations. Due to continued exposure, you are left no choice but to learn the flashcards permanently.

Unlike one-time tests like the FE exam, you can reuse your learned information for multiple conversations. In doing so, you are encouraging the acquisition of knowledge for long term usage instead of short term test scores.

The same logic applies to all three types of Absorbent Learning. Learning is an investment in yourself. It is not an affirmation of someone else's idea of success.

If children develop an interest in learning, they'll pay more attention in class, be less disruptive in and outside of school, avoid becoming a societal sickness, influence their *peers* to avoid becoming societal sicknesses, and influence their *peers' peers* to avoid becoming societal sicknesses.

At that point, there's hope society will someday be cured of its sickness.

Chapter 31

Chain Reaction

"How wonderful it is that nobody need wait a single moment before starting to improve the world."

— ANNE FRANK

While attending MBA school, I spent much of my class time (and free time) tinkering with a business idea. The idea centered around Visual Absorbent Learning. The plan was to consolidate people's personal learning goals and create posters they could display in their white spaces. It was to be a poster-peddling company with a grand vision to help educate the world (see the Visual Absorbent Learning section on wewanderpurposefully.com to see what this business idea eventually became).

Many of my MBA classes were focused on finding and exploiting the market for a product. I was tasked multiple times to identify the primary market for my hypothetical business. I struggled mightily to narrow my market down. I kept arguing my product was for everybody, and that narrowing my market would ostracize important market segments. Young adults like me should use it, teenagers should use it, parents should use it with their children, parents should use it for themselves, most everybody (who isn't blind) could benefit from Visual Absorbent Learning. These thoughts weren't much help in marketing classes whose main focus was delivering the right content to the right people, at the right time, and at the right place, in order to entice them to buy your product.

I started the PCT with my business idea still aimed at the impossibly broad market of everyone. It was not until I crossed the final miles into Canada when I realized who my primary market is:

<u>My market is people who love to learn.</u>

And people who love to learn come from all walks of life. These wonderful people exist, and if you've made it this far into this book, you are probably one of them. I appreciate you, and offer my congratulations for reading an entire book.

But don't get too excited now. You have homework to do. You are my target market, but *you* are not why I wrote this book. I did not write it for those who love learning, but for those who *ought* to love learning.

My dream is to see you bring my concepts to those who wouldn't even consider Absorbent Learning. Namely, those clueless man-on-the-street interviewees, those who don't have access to books, those who aren't interested in reading in general, those who think small knowledge is always trivial, or even your next door neighbor who is too proud to read a self-help book. Especially in this digital age, you have more influence over those around you than you think.

My thinking on this subject has been strongly influenced by the sociological work of PhD Harvardians Nicholas Christakis and James Fowler. I listened to their book *Connected* directly after the PCT as research for *Wander Purposefully*. Christakis and Fowler focus on just how far our personal influence can reach:

> Overall, we found that if you are a typical American, the probability that any two of your social contacts know each other, is about 52%. Although these measures characterize the networks we can see, they also tell us about the networks we cannot see.
> In the vast fabric of humanity, each person is connected to his friends, family, coworkers and neighbors, but these people are in turn connected to their friends, family, coworkers and neighbors, and so on endlessly into the distance until everyone on Earth is connected, pretty much, to everyone else, one way or another...
> It is this structural feature of networks that underlies the common expression "it's a small world"… each and every one of these ties offers opportunities to influence and be influenced.
> Students with studious roommates become more studious. Diners sitting next to heavy eaters eat more food. Homeowners with neighbors who garden wind up with manicured lawns. And this simple tendency for one person to influence another has tremendous consequences when we look beyond our immediate connections.
> Our friend's friend's friends affect us. It turns out that people do not copy only their friends, they also copy their friend's friends and their friend's friend's friends.

Not only are we highly connected to other people through our immediate connections, but, particularly through the recent power of social media, we are now hyper-connected to people with whom we have no immediate connection.

We might think our actions have little effect on the many. But we are dead wrong.

If you practice Absorbent Learning and take my applications to heart, you'll influence other people to practice Absorbent Learning. You'll even influence those well beyond your social reach.

Take my PCT experience for example. The first time I even considered a thru-hike occurred after my older brother Marshall hiked the 2,181-mile Appalachian Trail. Likewise, after I hiked the PCT, I inspired one of my friends to thru-hike it the following year. That friend announced his intention on social media, and his friends (who I do not know personally and thus are beyond my own social reach) were commenting about how they were inspired.

Not only do actions spread in this way, but, as Christakis and Fowler assert, so do emotions:

> If your friend feels happy, she smiles, you smile and, in the act of smiling, you also come to feel happy… People imitate the facial expressions of others, then, as a direct result, they come to feel as others do. This is called affective efference, or the facial feedback theory.

Affective efference is why we feel better after watching happy puppy videos. It is also why television networks use laugh tracks.

The Absorbent Learning lifestyle not only makes us smarter, more empathetic, more attractive, and more attuned — it also makes us happier.

Chapter 32

Happy

"This part of my life.. This little part.. Is called Happyness."
— **WILL SMITH**, THE PURSUIT OF HAPPYNESS

I listened to three books on trail whose main subject was happiness: Yale lawyer Gretchen Rubin's *The Happiness Project*, Douglas Carlton Adams' interview of the Dalai Lama & Archbishop Desmond Tutu known as *The Book of Joy*, and Harvard scholar Shawn Achor's *The Happiness Advantage*.

Gretchen Rubin's book details the author's attempts to make herself happier by embarking on a year-long quest to strengthen her own virtues. These virtues were mostly based upon a list of virtues from Benjamin Franklin's autobiography. Rubin provides an entertaining read. She gives the reader highly manicured, and practical, ways they can try to make themselves happier.

The Book of Joy is chock-full of Dalai Lama-isms, one of which is the following:

> "One great question underlies our existence… What is the purpose of life? After much consideration, I believe that the purpose of life is to find happiness. It does not matter whether one is a Buddhist like me, or a Christian like the Archbishop, or any other religion, or no religion at all. From the moment of birth, every human being wants to discover happiness and avoid suffering."

The book espouses a holistic view of life, and recommends meditational practices for its readers. I would prefer the Dalai Lama to put a greater emphasis on learning than meditation, but I can't argue with his stated opinion wherein happiness is the ultimate purpose of life.

The main focuses of Achor's book (one of my favorites) are the scientific and practical reasons why people should strive to make themselves and the people around them happy. His research includes over 200 studies, involving almost 275,000 people:

> Data abounds showing that happy workers have higher levels of productivity, produce higher sales, perform better in leadership positions, and receive higher performance ratings and higher pay. They also enjoy more job security and are less likely to take sick days, to quit, or to become burned out. Happy CEOs are more likely to lead teams of employees who are both happy and healthy, and who find their work climate conducive to high performance. The list of the benefits of happiness in the workplace goes on and on.

Achor does a great job at crystallizing the external incentives to be happy, and how being happy is beneficial for our personal life, our relationships, and our work.

All three of these books on happiness were best-sellers and have appealed to people far and wide. Taking the lessons of these books, there are three truths regarding human happiness.

1. We are always seeking practical ways to be happy.
2. The purpose of life is to be happy.
3. Being happy is to our advantage.

So how does Absorbent Learning make us happy? The answer is twofold.

First, it brightens the white space in your day. To illustrate this, let's check out the experiments performed by a superstar team of modern psychologists: Daniel Kahneman and Alan Krueger of Princeton University, Norbert Schwarz of the University of Michigan, David Schkade of the University of California San Diego, and Arthur Stone of Stony Brook University.

The researchers set out to create a way to measure the mental well-being of society. To do this, they gathered a voluminous sample of women, and studied their emotional well-being throughout the day by taking note of when and whether the women were experiencing positive or negative emotions. Using degrees of positive feelings (like joy, hope, and amusement) and degrees of negative feelings (like anger, depression, and loneliness), the researchers were able to quantify how much of a specific person's day was spent in an unhappy state. They called this quantification the "U-Index." They calculated the U-index by taking the amount of time spent in an unpleasant mood, dividing that time by the total waking hours of a person's day, and slapping a percent sign at the end of the quotient. For example, if a subject spent 5 hours of a 20 hour waking day in an unpleasant mood, that person would have a U-index of 25%.

Not only did the experimenters set out to define a specific test subject's personal U-index, but they also sought to define the U-index for specific activities. Thus, they found the U-index of a morning commute to be 29%, of work to be 27%, of child care to be 24%, and so on.

Daniel Kahneman's *Thinking, Fast and Slow* describes the ultimate conclusions of this experiment to be as follows:

> The mood of the moment depends primarily on the current situation. Mood at work, for example, is largely unaffected by the factors that influence general job satisfaction, including benefits and status. More important are situational factors… Our emotional state is largely determined by what we attend to, and we are normally focused on our current activity…
>
> The use of time is one of the areas of life over which people have some control. Few individuals can will themselves to have a sunnier disposition, but some may be able to arrange their lives to spend less of their day commuting, and more time doing things they enjoy.

This sets up the first way Absorbent Learning can make you happy. If you are using Absorbent Learning during a mindless job you hate, you will hate your job a little less. Maybe you look down from your computer screen and look at a coffee mug on your desk displaying constellations you want to memorize. If you hate commuting, but begin to listen to an audiobook you enjoy during your commute, you will hate your commute a little less. If you loathe exercising, but are multitasking while suffering through a workout, you will be more predisposed to like exercising.

By creating this small oasis-like atmosphere of growth within a desert of dissatisfaction, you gain a feeling of productiveness you wouldn't have had otherwise.

You could have a day that felt wasted and purposeless at work, but at the very least, you know a little more about constellations, or you listened to an audiobook. Knowing where Orion's Belt is or finishing an audiobook are real, tangible accomplishments because they have the potential to serendipitously benefit you in the future.

If you truly enjoy being productive, you will look *forward* to the jobs, workouts, and commutes you previously hated. Your negative emotional states will be transformed, not just into neutral emotional states, but into *positive* emotional states. It's like the 14 point momentum swing that happens when your football team intercepts a pass in your own end zone, and returns it to the opposite end zone for the pick 6. Introducing Absorbent Learning can reduce your U-Index significantly, thus making your day objectively happier.

The second, most compelling, reason why Absorbent Learning makes you happier is the attunement to others which results in the easier formation of weak ties.

For me, Jenny started as a stranger at the Star Bar. She was more easily converted into a weak tie because of my Absorbent Learning. She has since transformed into the strongest tie of my life.

Through Absorbent Learning, it is easier to create weak ties out of strangers. Those weak ties have the potential to become strong ties. Strong ties are the foundations upon which our happiness is built.

The times spent with strong ties are the most rewarding, and purpose-filled, of our lives. This is not an uncommon notion. It's why blockbuster movies are oftentimes centered around the protagonist striving to save their loved ones from harm.

Time spent with our loved ones are also the happiest times of our lives.

Being happy, according to psychological experiments referred to by Shawn Achor and Martin Seligman, has also been found to prolong your life. The longer you live, the longer you can spend time with loved ones, and the more happy moments you can share with them.

As one of the more tragic of Chris McCandless' pre-death etchings captured in *Into The Wild* said: "Happiness only real when shared."

Chapter 33

The Thought Cascade

"Luminous beings are we! Not this crude matter!"

— YODA, THE EMPIRE STRIKES BACK

Wander Purposefully includes many references to outside sources, namely the audiobooks I listened to on the PCT. I supplied my entire reading list back in Part 1 of this book so you could see exactly how much of this book was derived from my PCT PhD. Though I poke fun at Ivy League PhDs in this book, I recognize that, as Isaac Newton said when speaking of his own accomplishments, "If I have seen further, it is by standing on the shoulders of giants." I am grateful for those giants who shared their studies and ideas with me in their books. They taught me, helped spark my own thoughts, and eventually led to this book.

Alternatively, I could have acted as if the ideas presented in *Wander Purposefully* were the result of my own thoughts alone. By doing so, however, I would undermine one of my biggest objectives: to encourage Auditory Absorbent Learning. If one of my goals was to convince readers to read more, precisely because it triggers more thought, why would I edit out references to authors who triggered my own thoughts? Listening to authors in my white space triggered epiphanies during my immense amount of white space time on the PCT.

Consider what thought is exactly: it is the result of billions of individual primings brought about by the unique perspective of your upbringing, paired with your own personal experiences.

As I discussed during the parallax chapters of this book, you are influenced and primed since birth to think the way you do. Every single thought you have is a logical flowchart whose progression was influenced by your unique circumstances, and your unique reaction to those circumstances.

Thought is linear. What you think about next directly follows what you thought about right before. Therefore, in order to lengthen the extension of our linear thought to reach new revelations, in order to create *original* thought, we need to increase the *quantity* of our thoughts.

In other words, we need to *learn*. If we don't learn, we have no option but to think the same thoughts we've already thought in an endless loop.

If we don't seek learning, our thought extension can only be lengthened by chance, within the bay of our own experiences.

My thinking on this matter has been greatly influenced by Bill Bryson's impeccably researched book *A Short History of Almost Everything*. This was the first book I listened to when I was at the Mexican border about to embark on a long walk to Canada. I listened to it for a second time as my final research for this book. I recommend you read it, especially if you like science, history, or both.

A good example of how our thought is linear comes from Bryson's explanation of theoretical and experimental physics. The following is not to explain how atomic theory works, but to point out how the progression of thought builds upon itself.

- John Dalton (Born 1856) proposed that all matter is composed of indivisible atoms.
- J.J. Thomson (Born the same year as Dalton) disproved part of John Dalton's hypothesis, and then proposed the shape of an atom to resemble raisin pudding, a ball of matter with electrons inside it.
- Hantaro Nagaoka (Born 1865, 9 years after Dalton and Thomson) proposed an atomic model wherein electrons revolve around a nucleus.
- Ernest Rutherford (Born 1871, 6 years after Nagaoka) disproved J.J. Thomson's raisin pudding theory, and proved the existence of Nagaoka's nucleus.
- Otto Hahn (Born 1879, 8 years after Rutherford) discovered proof of the possibility of nuclear fission (the splitting of an atom's nucleus).
- Enrico Fermi (Born 1901, 22 years after Hahn) developed the nuclear reactor, building on Otto Hahn's fission idea.
- It is at this point where the thoughts leading up to the mid 1940's became lethal. As Bryson says: "Scientists had reached a point where they understood the atom at an extremely profound level — as they all too effectively demonstrated in August 1945, by exploding a pair of atomic bombs over Japan."

The subsequent scientific discoveries of the atomic theory all build off, expand on, or disprove the thoughts of previous contributors. So, also, do our own thoughts cascade linearly.

If *Wander Purposefully* inspires you to seek learning, thus jumpstarting a cascade of thought, that cascade may lead to truly original thought. This could be a new idea, invention, book, movie, or anything else.

If you are developing your own original thoughts, keep the following ten historical anecdotes, sourced from Bryson's *A Short History of Nearly Everything*, in mind as you continue in your learning.

1. Sometimes people don't pay attention. The popular current theory wherein Earth's moon originated as a direct result of an impact between Earth and a large asteroid has been assumed to be a very recent one. In reality, the theory was proposed back in the 1940s by a Harvard man named Reginald Daley. His theory did not gain any traction, and was quickly forgotten.

2. Sometimes people actually *do* pay attention, as Isaac Newton experienced after his *Principia* was published. *Principia* established the laws of physics and gravity as we know them (later elaborated upon by Albert Einstein). After the publishing of *Principia*, Newton was immediately recognized as the greatest scientific man of his era. He was the first scientist ever to be knighted in Britain.

3. Sometimes great original thought is not deemed economically valuable by those in power, and an author needs a lucky break for his work to be noticed. Edmund Halley (of Halley's Comet) is responsible for the publishing of Newton's *Principia*:

    > The Royal Society had promised to publish [*Principia*], but now pulled out, citing financial embarrassment. The year before, the Society had backed a costly flop called *The History of Fishes*, and they now suspected that the market for a book on mathematical principles would be less than clamorous. Halley, whose means were not great, paid for the book's publication out of his own pocket.

4. Sometimes "crackpot" theorists gain traction. Look no further than Pythagoras, Socrates, Jesus, Luther, Copernicus, Galileo, and Darwin. During their lives, these men were persecuted for their theories by the (often religious) authorities who were on the supposed moral high ground. Just because you are in the majority doesn't mean you are correct.

5. Sometimes an idea is ridiculed because the world is not yet ready for it, as was the case with John Newlands' periodic table:

> The principle [of a periodic table] had actually been anticipated three years previously by an amateur chemist in England named John Newlands. He suggested that when elements were arranged by weight they appeared to repeat certain properties...at every eighth place along the scale.

> Newlands had compared the table to musical octaves which also repeat every eight whole notes. Because of this, he was widely ridiculed and denounced amongst his peers who thought his Law to be preposterous. Dmitri Mendeleev came along a few years later, used the same basic methodology as Newlands, and was quickly pronounced brilliant. The scientific world reveres him to this day.

6. People have gone to enormous lengths to establish original thought, as in the case of Richard Norwood:

> Norwood, whose first love was trigonometry and thus, angles, decided to bring a little mathematical rigor to navigation, and to that end, he determined to calculate the length of a degree.

> Starting with his back against the tower of London, Norwood spent two devoted years marching 280 miles north to York. Repeatedly stretching and measuring a length of chain as he went, all the while making the most meticulous adjustments for the rise and fall of the land, and the meanderings of the road.

7. Sometimes original thought comes at great sacrifice and real danger for thinkers:

    > In America, Benjamin Franklin famously risked his life by flying a kite in an electrical storm. In France, a chemist named Pilâtre de Rozier tested the flammability of hydrogen by gulping a mouthful and blowing across an open flame, proving at a stroke that hydrogen is indeed explosively combustible, and that eyebrows are not necessarily a permanent feature of one's face.

8. Sometimes people had to die for progress to be made. The prominence of the denier can be a great inhibitor of progress, as was the case with Lord Kelvin (of the Kelvin Temperature Scale) and Dmitri Mendeleev (of the periodic table). As these legendary scientists advanced in age, they became irresolute and unmoving on theories of theirs that had long since been proven incorrect. This can be somewhat expected, as the natural response to the refutation of one's life work is almost always rancorous.

9. Sometimes we make catastrophically bad assumptions, but do not realize it until too late, as was the case with lead poisoning. Initial health testing on lead only tested urine and feces for health abnor-

malities. Little did we know, lead deposits actually manifest themselves in the bones and blood, both of which were not tested at all. This had disastrous, lethal consequences.

10. Last, but not least, be humble. Acting like a know-it-all oftentimes turns out to be more ignorant than ignorance itself.

Chapter 34

The Knowledge Drop

"A gentleman is someone who can play the accordion, but doesn't."

— TOM WAITS

In everyday situations, the only thing worse than someone who knows nothing is someone who knows everything, but cannot filter it appropriately. The Smart Aleck, the wise guy, the cocksure prophet — all generally obnoxious. These labels can seriously undermine the effectiveness of the relational advantages provided by Absorbent Learning.

Here, the art of conversation truly becomes important. Upstaging or one-upping your peers is not always beneficial, especially if it is unintentional. It is important to realize your knowledge does not always have a place in the conversation.

The knowledge drop can be tricky because you should be proud to show off your knowledge. You've prepared for months and years with the belief that when the opportunity comes, your practice will pay off. There have been plenty of times where I've dropped knowledge at an ill-opportune time in the conversation. Plenty of times where my knowledge sounded too braggy. What I've discovered is you have to tiptoe the asymptotic line of being a know-it-all.

The art of conversation is finicky, and, just like everything else, requires practice. You need to spend time in these situations to fully grasp the times when you should drop the knowledge, and when you should keep the knowledge to yourself. If travel comes up in conversation, you don't *need* to tell your conversant that you know all the countries and capitals on earth, even if you are proud of that achievement.

Dale Carnegie dispensed many nuggets of wisdom in his classic book *How to Win Friends and Influence People*. One of his most potent thoughts read: "You can make more friends in two months by becoming genuinely interested in other people, than you can in two years by trying to get other people interested in you."

Focus on your conversant's aspirations, and, as the conversation progresses, you could possibly mention your past experience to lend context to your comments. The key is to be *invited* to share your knowledge. This invitation may or may not be subtly coaxed by your own conversation tactics, but until you've been invited, don't drop the knowledge.

The root word for humility (the Latin "*humus*") literally means soil. Thus, to be humble is to liken oneself to the dirt beneath your feet.

Conclusion

CONCLUSION

Chapter 35

Summarization

Though experiments about the techniques I've introduced in *Wander Purposefully* could conceivably be conducted, I will not spend five years of my time getting a "real" PhD, and then X more years conducting the experiments to gather "conclusive evidence" before publishing this book.

A single experiment, say putting a periodic table in front of a 9-year-old, and then observing its effects, would have to span years in order to give the 9-year-old time to repeatedly expose themselves to information. Even if you could organize this experiment, there would be a huge Hawthorne Effect skew in any data gathered. As you'll recall, the Hawthorne Effect stems from the intentional actions performed by a test subject due to their awareness of a tester's presence.

How do you go about measuring serendipity and one's preparedness for it? It's impossible. It's a waste of my time, and, most importantly, a waste of *our* time.

I've taken Absorbent Learning to the extreme in my life. I am anecdotal proof of the validity of Absorbent Learning. That is more than enough proof for me to be motivated to share my experiences with you. It was my intention to create a book that was neither contrived nor affectatious, to provide a logical argument, and a corporeal example, to convince readers to take their learning to the next level.

I truly believe in Absorbent Learning and its beneficial effects for the self and society.

Three of the main beneficial effects for the self are as follows:

1. If you acquire more knowledge, you become more worldly, personable, and interesting.
2. Being worldly, personable, and interesting are universally desirable and attractive qualities.
3. Having desirable qualities is beneficial in many areas of life.

Three of the main beneficial effects for society are as follows:

1. The ability to be empathetic towards various perspectives allows you to easily connect with people different from yourself.
2. If a person can connect easier with other people, less disrespect, violence, and conflicts will arise.
3. A brilliant cascade of original thought could lead to world-altering ideas.

Chapter 36

Dream On

"If you will it Dude, it is no dream."
— **WALTER SOBCHAK**, THE BIG LEBOWSKI

If your dreams are undefined, learn anything and everything you can until inspiration strikes. Knowing what you want to do with your life means you would do it even if you were rich, and didn't have to do it. You would do illogical things just for the sake of doing them. You would love what you do. If I won the lottery, I would still write this book.

If your dreams are clear, focus on learning everything you can pertaining to your dream, and seek out the opportunities to make your preparation pay off. From Roman philosopher Seneca: "Luck is what happens when preparation meets opportunity." You are the hero, and the villain, of your own story.

Within your learning, your dreams may change for the better. I started the PCT with a dream of starting my own business. I ended the PCT with the outline for this book.

Along your Absorbent Learning journey, do not forget morality.

If you achieve a personal goal, are you now automatically a good person?
No.

If you've earned a PhD, are you now automatically a good person?
Definitely not.

If you've hiked the PCT and listened to 71 books during it, does that automatically make you a good person?
Alas, no.

Are these identities meaningless? Should people give up on their goals? Absolutely not. If you achieve your goals, find ways to help others achieve theirs. Use your platform to make a lasting impression on other people's lives, not just your own.

This book is my own attempt to make a lasting impression on your life.

I am an example of a kid who took full advantage of my many opportunities in the rat race of today's society. Because of this, I can afford to spend months hiking and writing. Maybe, through this writing, I will have rectified my own cognitive dissonance regarding the relative ease in which I achieved success.

Contradictory Statement #1: I had many opportunities handed to me.
Contradictory Statement #2: Many people are not presented with these same opportunities.

Chapter 37

The Wager

"It's a dangerous business, Frodo, going out your door. You step onto the road, and if you don't keep your feet, there's no knowing where you might be swept off to."
— **J.R.R. TOLKIEN**, THE FELLOWSHIP OF THE RING

You do not know where your new knowledge will take you, or how Absorbent Learning will affect your life. What you do know is *knowing more things has limitless beneficial potential.*

It's never bad to have listened to a book that informs and expands your thought processes.

It's never bad to memorize something that's hard to memorize.
It's never bad to learn how to understand someone else's point of view.

CONCLUSION

These are examples of tangible things you can do to make yourself unique. They are attainable if you prioritize and intentionally work at it.

The concept of Pascal's Wager is exceedingly appropriate when deciding whether or not to engage in Absorbent Learning.

Blaise Pascal, famed 17th century philosopher and physicist, postulated if you must be incorrect about the existence of God, then you are much better off believing in him and being wrong, than *not* believing in him and being wrong. Thus, instead of eternal damnation, your worst consequence would be the foregoing of a few fleeting earthly pleasures.

Although many deservedly criticize Pascal's wager as a legitimate defense of faith, it is an effective metaphor for Absorbent Learning.

Like Pascal's Wager, Absorbent Learning is all upside with no downside. It's a no risk, big reward, investment. It's like your 15th round sleeper fantasy football draft pick becoming your MVP.

Chapter 38

Wander Purposefully

"Dost thou love life? Then do not squander time, for that's the stuff life is made of."
—**BENJAMIN FRANKLIN**, POOR RICHARD'S ALMANACK

It does not matter what you do outside of your white spaces. Maybe you're a garbage man, a pediatrician, a stay-at-home parent, an electrician, or unemployed. What connects us all is the existence of white space. What differentiates us is what we do during our white space.

Think about the white spaces in your day. I've spent this book convincing you to look at those times through a different lens. No longer are they negative values on Daniel Kahneman's U-Index. No longer should your mind wander aimlessly in your white space.

These times now take shape: no longer as wastes of time, but as ripe opportunities to learn.

The idiom "spending time" is poignantly symbolic. It ties the idea of infinite time to the finiteness of money. Just as we are certain to run out of money if we spend too much, it is also certain that, upon our inevitable deaths, we will run out of time. As such, time should be valued with the same urgency we give to money. This shouldn't be a depressing thought; rather, it should be emboldening. It should give you the rationalization you need to step out of the routines that are not giving your life purpose. The same person who willingly spends most of their waking hours going to work to build someone's else's dream, also doesn't see the need to learn enough to be able to pursue their own dreams. You could get hit by a bus tomorrow. Do what you need to do today.

A wise man once told me: "If you're pissed off about how much you're being taxed, go make more money." In the same way, if we are angry about how much time we spend doing things we don't want to do, go make more time. Absorbent Learning makes bonus time of the white space time we thought was unusable.

Never in history has it been this easy to learn. Never has technology afforded us so much white space. Never have we had the technology to fully take advantage of white space.

Google and Wikipedia have put the world's knowledge at our fingertips.

Audiobooks, an invention of the last half century, are now available to us at the swipe of a finger.

I can jump on a plane and be on the other side of the world in half a day.

Knowledge is instantly attainable, and considering how long it took humankind to achieve this, it is a damn shame if we don't take advantage of it.

Through reading this book, the popular paradigms that white space is unimportant, and trivial information is trivial, have hopefully been shattered. You may also be experiencing your own cognitive dissonance regarding your current actions. These might be your current thoughts:

Contradictory Statement #1: I should be using Absorbent Learning in my white space.
Contradictory Statement #2: I am currently doing nothing in my white space.

Remember, to produce an uncomfortable feeling, cognitive dissonance involves an intentional choice, and a perceived negative consequence resulting from that choice. The negative consequence of wasting your white space is your failure to benefit from Absorbent Learning.

I have bad news for you that's actually good news. The fact you know you could be using your white space more productively, but are now consciously choosing to do otherwise, should motivate you to change your actions for the better. You now know about it, so the only thing stopping you is, likely, laziness.

White space is time *waiting* to be used.

Focus on your learning goals. Where once was itinerant nothingness, ambition now dwells. Your mind will no longer wander aimlessly unless you *let* it wander aimlessly. You can choose to wander purposefully within your life's white space.

> Absorbent Learning is a lifestyle.
> It helps build your character.
> It replaces non-experience with *some* experience.
> It takes advantage of humanity's heuristics.
> It helps you attune to strangers and find new friends via homophily.
> It helps you make your existing friendships stronger.
> It helps you serendipitously attract significant others.
> By turning your bays into estuaries, it gives you the ability to see the world

in a parallactic way.

It helps aid your decision-making in personal situations of cognitive dissonance.

Through social norms, it promotes love amongst strangers.

It makes you, and those around you, happier.

It helps you to love learning.

In doing all of this, Absorbent Learning perpetuates your own self interests, and makes the world a better place. You don't need to make room in your busy day to start, because the room already exists as white space.

Anyone can wander purposefully.

Everyone *should* wander purposefully. So…

WHAT ARE YOU WAITING FOR?

Epilogue

The Stans and You: A Love Song, The Last Stan

Before the trail diary appendix, we will visit with the Stans one last time. Kazakhstan, Kyrgyzstan, Tajikistan, Uzbekistan, Turkmenistan.

Peruse the map, and vocalize the names of the countries. Take in their position relative to one another. Remember to use context. Kazakh and Russian Cossacks. Turkmenistan is the closest to Turkey. Take the easy wins. Kazakhstan is the big one. Remember your patterns and recall the clockwise KTUT-King Tut mnemonic device.

Now turn the page.

Test yourself with the blank map. See if you can correctly identify each Stan.

Do you know the Stans now? My bet is, if you don't yet, you are well on your way. Depending on your Stan proficiency prior to reading this book, you've cared about the Stans approximately 3 times.

Imagine if you put a map in one of your white spaces and looked at it every day. It doesn't seem so daunting, does it?

The only thing left to do, if geography is your cup of tea, is to get yourself a new map, post it in a white space, and intentionally look at it every day. Just like we did with the Stans, start working on Central America, the Balkan Peninsula, Indochina, the Canadian Provinces, the African continent, and so on. Eventually, just like a song you listen to over and over again, you'll know them by heart. They've been waiting for you for your entire life. A perfect love song. The Stans and you. Together forever.

Appendix

Trail Diary

The excruciating minutiae of trail life. This part of the book will be much more informal than it has been up to this point.

Upon re-reading my diary, I've realized I wrote more about things that satisfied my intense cravings for beds and food, than about the audiobooks I listened to or the actual day-to-day hiking I did. Most of the notes about my audiobooks are contained on the bookmarks in my Audible App, not in this diary.

I also namedrop a lot. Sometimes I will namedrop a person and they will never be mentioned again. That is the nature of the trail. You meet someone on a given day and there is a great chance you will never see that person ever again. They could be hiking faster or slower than you, they could get injured or quit, or they could take a couple zero days and never catch up. As you'll probably notice, it truly took a village to get me from Mexico to Canada.

The writing style also changes along the journey. This is mainly because my mother started requesting pictures of my trail diary so she and my dad could read it and follow along. The first thirty or so days are written as more of a terse stream-of-consciousness chronicle intended for my own reminiscing, whereas later it starts to turn more into a narrative for the benefit of my parents. I had no idea this would one day be published, so I didn't put too much eloquence into it. You may notice I did not have the best attitude at some points. This can probably be chalked up to how uncomfortable I was. This was my first backpacking trip longer than two days. In retrospect, my writing should have taken on a much more grateful tone. I recognize there are many people who would love to do something like the PCT, but do not have the means, ability, opportunity, or freedom to do so. I am extremely fortunate.

Looking back, I regret focusing on some parts of the trail experience while completely neglecting other parts. For example, I notice I barely ever describe my trail food, but *never* fail to describe the food I got at restaurants in town. I didn't even want to think about my trail food, let alone write about it. From this diary, you may think the trail is full of cheeseburgers, milkshakes, and other tasty vittles. Sadly, in reality, it was mostly trail mix, ramen noodles, and beef jerky.

There are also a few main characters that recur frequently:

- Eddie — My best friend and hiking partner.
- Marshall — One of my older brothers. He hiked about half of the trail with me.
- Jenny — My girlfriend. I introduced her in the beginning of the book.
- John — Another of my older brothers who hiked with us for a week.

In case you are not familiar with trail jargon, here is a brief glossary of common hiking terms, which can also be found on the PCT section of wewanderpurposefully.com, alongside a map of the PCT:

- AT — Short for Appalachian Trail, a long distance hiking trail similar to

- the PCT located on the Atlantic United States seaboard
- Bear Can (AKA Bear Cannister) — An indestructible plastic drum to put your food in to protect against curious bears.
- Burn — A section of the trail a fire burned in years past. The trees are all dead.
- Cowboy Camping — Sleeping outside without a tent, as cowboys would.
- Guthook — A very effective smartphone app used for trail navigation and pathfinding.
- Hiker Trash — An affectionate term used to describe particularly unkempt hikers.
- Hitch — An abbreviation for hitch hike.
- KT Tape (AKA Kinesiology Tape) — An elastic pain-relief tape found in sporting goods stores that I found to be especially effective. I refer to it as witchcraft tape because I didn't understand how it worked.
- Nero Day (AKA "nero") — A nero day is basically a half-day. It's a day you hike *near* zero trail miles. This could mean you hike 1, or 2, or even 10+ miles, but you only hike part of the day.
- Nobo — Short for northbound. A Nobo PCT hiker starts in Mexico and heads north to Canada.
- PR — short for Personal Record.
- Ruck — In noun form, ruck refers to a hiker's backpack.
- Slackpacking — Hiking without your full backpack. Presumably someone will be meeting you later with your full pack. Normally, a slackpack only contains food, water, and first aid emergency supplies.
- Sobo — Short for southbound. A Sobo PCT hiker starts in Canada and heads south to Mexico.
- Talus — A talus section of trail is tough to walk on because the trail itself is composed of talus rock. Talus rock is usually sharp, jagged, and painful to walk on.

- Trail Angel — A person who provides Trail Magic.
- Trail Family — A group of people who hike together for an extended period of time.
- Trail Magic — When a complete stranger does something kind for you.
- Vortex — Used when referring to a place that is so awesome, you struggle to leave to go back to the trail.
- Yogi — To Yogi is to ask a stranger for something. Most of the time a hiker Yogi's water off of dayhikers who have extra.
- Zero Day (AKA "zero") — A zero day is a day in which zero trail miles were hiked. It is a day off.

In the interest of keeping the diary authentic, I have mostly resisted the urge to edit any poorly written prose. I contradict myself sometimes, frequently confuse verb tenses, and often use the same adjectives over and over. I do not explain trail jargon within the text, and I namedrop geographical trail landmarks with no prior explanation. I found it a strange challenge to type out (and narrate) this diary, because my thoughts sometimes jump all over the place in run-on sentences with little transition. Consequently, it may sound janky, monotone, or stilted at points.

The diary is, by and large, exactly how I wrote it. Most of the time, from within my tent, I would scribble into my dirty gray journal with my waterproof pen at the end of the long day. Sometimes, I would fall behind and need to recall 3-4 days of feelings and actions in a single writing session. I redacted a few parts too personal to share, but most of it is as follows:

DAY 1

Drove down to Campo with my parents. Met a guy named Jared at the start, would meet up with him later. Met Kathleen from Ballard there too. Started down trail, first notable thing happened about 2 miles in. Big rattlesnake about 1-2 feet from the trail!! It rattled loudly while Eddie was walking by, I chose to go off trail to avoid it. We stopped near noon and got back going at 2. We met Jared again around 3. I had a blister hotspot developing, so he washed my foot and treated it for a blister. I gave him the trail name Jesus because of the foot washing. He is a wealth of knowledge. I got some serious cramps in my right quad at the end of the day and had to stop. We camped 12 miles in.

DAY 2

Got up at 5 and summitted Hauser by 12. We ran out of water about a mile from Lake Morena and were dreaming of the Malt Shop there where there'd be ice water. My nose started bleeding randomly without any provocation, as if in protest to my strange surroundings. It's been about 80 degrees, which has seemed crazy hot, but we're lucky it's not hotter here in the desert.

DAY 3

We got up at like 5 but didn't leave til 7 because we were waiting for Jesus and Crunch to get ready. Crunch is a Swiss programmer who retired after selling his company and mining bitcoins since 2011. He looks about 30 years old! He said he bought a $150,000 supercomputer. We left and made great time and stopped at a campground for lunch. We lunched with Alyssa and an old guy who must've been at least 75 who hiked the AT last year.

DAY 4

We stayed at Cibbets last night and hiked up 2500 feet of elevation up to Mount Laguna. We walked to the cafe and got an enormous burger and mac and cheese where the chef just put whatever he wanted on it. We decided to stay in a motel to get a good night of sleep. When I walked in the door I stepped on a crunchy beetle. It was gross.

DAY 5

Slept okay at motel, we woke up late and had breakfast at Blue Jay lodge and hung out until 9:30. We hit the road and saw incredible views of the Anza-Borrego National Park. Edd climbed out on a ledge and I took an awesome pic. Incredible windy day with gusts up to 100 mph. We almost cowboy camped in the valley. I was a good Samaritan and told everyone about the good camping spot.

DAY 6

Jesus caught up to us during the night and convinced us to hike 21 (!!!!!) miles to Scissor crossing. Today was definitely the hardest day of the trail so far. We were pooped and out of water with 5 miles to go but persevered. My first hitchhiking experience was very positive. The first person we flagged pulled over and took us to our Inn, the Oak Hill Inn. Incredible value for 2 nights at $150. We are taking a zero day tomorrow to rest our aching joints. Well deserved and good timing because it is going to rain.

DAY 7

Zero day. And on the 7th day they rested. Laundry, food, and we are sending our bear cans on to Kennedy Meadows to shed weight.

DAY 8

Bill from Oak Hill Inn gave us a ride to the trail so we didn't have to hitchhike. Really interesting guy who built the majority of his house by himself and lived in Kauai for a little bit. The hike today was pretty uneventful save for a stray bee stinging Eddie's back and my joints hurting more than they ought to after a zero day. We did 16 miles and aiming for Warner Springs tomorrow night.

DAY 9

Incredibly scenic day of hiking on our way to Warner Springs. Cows, meadows, gnarly trees, and Eagle Rock. Warner Springs was like a refugee camp. We did "bucket" showers which was literally just pouring a bucket of cold water on ourselves. Hung out with Old Steve, Bryson, Pot Hole, and Kitchen Sink. I'm starting to notice that hiking this trail is me always trying to walk TO somewhere, the next destination is always farther up down the trail. I pass by things just once. I'm never walking BACK from somewhere, just TO somewhere. As a rule, the journey to somewhere always feels much longer than the way back. If there isn't a scientific term or study confirming this, there should be. The last mile before Warner Springs felt like it took forever.

DAY 10

Hiking is getting tough, hot and hilly today. Trying to make it to "Mike's Place" tonight.

DAY 11

Mike's place last night was good but we got in after sundown so everyone was almost going to bed. Atta Girl and Scott made us some bomb pizza. We woke up kinda late and got goin. We both forgot our headphones in our camp shorts and didn't want to unpack so we didn't hike with headphones. I've realized that headphones are a huge morale boost for me. The 10 miles to Tule Spring were difficult. When we got there, there were 6 or 7 other hikers there already. We broke out the guitar and filtered the streamwater.

DAY 12

My birthday! We spent last night at the top of the mountain. Eddie felt the urge to make a campfire, but I was completely exhausted. We had to hike 10 miles to Paradise Cafe. We stopped at Mary's place and talked to Manbrodude and sent mother's day postcards to our moms. We called Paradise Cafe once we got to the highway. We were picked up by a woman who ended up being our waitress 5 minutes later. We got there and Pothole, Bryson, Atta Girl, Steve, Chris, and Gabe were there. They started calling me Cash when I got there because I was singing *Folsom Prison Blues* the day before. I don't like that trail name, so I won't be keeping it. I think I'll go by Red instead. Jesus called me that after the nosebleed I got on day 2. I ordered bacon & eggs, a lemonade, a milkshake, and a beer, then we hung out for a couple hours to wait until my parents came. My parents came and I ordered the Bambino sandwich for lunch. We headed to the

Ledwick's after lunch and mom did our laundry and we hung out with my dad for a couple hours. I asked him a lot about his past that I never knew before. He was drafted when he was 26 and spent a year in Vietnam. We had lasagna and banana cake for my bday dinner. It was really nice. The Ledwicks came home about 9:30 PM after their play and I got to hang out with the kids for a little and Jessica and Mike. I could barely walk today because of my left foot. It's very swollen and I am concerned.

DAY 13

Our second zero day. Everything coming up roses today. Mike drove us to Anza Post Office to pick up our food packages then drove us back to Paradise Cafe. That was really nice of him. We got breakfast and hung out with Alyssa, Leap Frog, and Calvin. A guy named The Viking who says he was the voice coach for Metallica offered to drive us to Idyllwild because of the fire closure. Free! I also stupidly forgot my trekking poles in mom's car and so called ConJon and he overnighted new ones to Idyllwild Post Office free of charge. We will have to pick them up tomorrow. Eddie, Leap Frog, and I are staying at an awesome cheap motel called Silver Pines tonight. I get my own bed all to myself for the first time this whole trip.

DAY 14

We decided to take another zero day in Idyllwild for a few reasons: My left foot was still swollen, my trekking poles didn't arrive until 1 pm, and we weren't going to get an early start anyways. We spent a lazy day where we watched TV while I iced and elevated my foot. We are getting a shuttle at 6 AM tomorrow to go back to the trail. I cut up the tongues of my shoes to give my feet some breathing room. Hopefully these modifications help with my foot pain.

DAY 15

Caught the 6 AM shuttle to Deer Springs trail and were immediately greeted with about 2,000 feet of elevation over a couple miles. We got lost for the first time today after taking a wrong turn at a poorly marked intersection. We had to clamber upwards on loose gravel for a while to get back to the trail. I heard a story about Gabe where he found a big pinecone and wanted to ship it home for a souvenir. He decided to buy a gallon of ice cream because he thought the container would be an ideal shipping container for the pinecone. So he ate the whole gallon of ice cream before realizing that the pinecone was bigger than the gallon. It was slow going at first today because we had two zero days in Idyllwild. We only went 14 miles, but tomorrow is all downhill. We are thinking of staying in Cabazon to go to the In N Out there. Listened mostly to *A Walk in the Woods* by Bill Bryson today.

DAY 16

Probably the hardest hiking day thus far, really gave Scissor Crossing day a run for its money. 18 miles mostly downhill but really hot. Culminated with a 4 mile desert stretch to highway 10 that was brutal. Eddie got stung by a bee again, this time on the chin. We got to the underpass and our day took a turn for the better. A trail angel gave us soda and water and drove us to the Stagecoach Motor Inn in Banning. We showered up and Ubered to the Cabazon In n Out where we feasted like kings. Double Doubles and fries, and shakes. We went to Panda Express directly after In N Out and ate again. Best sleep yet on the trail with a king bed and AC.

DAY 17

We slept in til 9 AM and got to the trail at 10:30. We passed the In N Out on our way to the trail and I seriously regretted not stopping there for a late breakfast. We walked just 9 miles today and ended in Whitewater Preserve. Great wading pool and very scenic.

DAY 18

Tough day. 17 miles all uphill. Unique to this day was the seven or eight river crossings throughout the day. We followed the river through a canyon through the San Gorgonio Wilderness. Chris hiked near us for a good portion of the day. We got to the campsite very late and so were stuck with sloped tents. My sleeping pad sprung a leak and deflated, so I slept on the ground.

DAY 19

Got up and decided to hike just 13 miles, though most were uphill. Eddie and I had a somewhat heated debate about whether to go to Big Bear tomorrow or not. I cannot stop craving breakfast food. As soon as I can I will order 3 over easy eggs, 4 pieces of bacon, hash browns, double toast, fruit, milk and OJ. Hopefully in 2 mornings.

DAY 20

We forced ourselves to get up at 4:45 AM to get an early start of the 18 miles to cover. This ended up being our most efficient day yet. We covered 18 miles before 3 PM! We hitched into town with a mechanic named John. We checked into the Big Bear hostel and a brash, lazy guy named Sarge showed us around.

We then went to Jasper's Steakhouse and got huge "cheeseburgers" that used whole grilled cheese sandwiches instead of buns. Immediately put me in a food coma and went straight to bed.

DAY 21

Zero day in Big Bear Lake. Got an average breakfast and a good lunch. Went to Big 5 to buy new air mattress and did laundry. Took care of some logistics for Friday's Lake Arrowhead meeting with Jenny!!!

DAY 22

Got up around 6 and headed to Grizzly Manor Cafe for breakfast. I ordered the Mysterious "Hot Mess" which ended up being a huge scramble. Afterwards I had big stomach issues and had to take some Metamucil and Calmoseptine. No Bueno. We decided to hike around the lake and take Cougar Crest up to the PCT. We did 14 miles total. Once we got to a campground I climbed up a big hill to try and get service to Facetime Jenny. I fell on the way up and majorly scraped my hand. Luckily I have KT (witchcraft) tape that heals everything.

DAY 23

Today is Thursday and we are to meet Jenny and Marshall tomorrow afternoon, but we are only 8 miles from Arrowhead. Therefore we are going to push past Arrowhead and have them pick us up past it. Not going to lie, it was very tempting to go straight to Arrowhead but we are already taking 2.5 zeroes this weekend and a third would have been egregious. We saw TWO rattlesnakes in the middle of the trail today. We waited til they slithered out of sight. Makes you wonder how many rattlers are nearby that we can't see. Deep Creek Hot

Springs tomorrow and Arrowhead!!!!

DAY 24

We got up early and visited Deep Creek Hot Springs at around 7:30 and left at 10:30. Extremely picturesque pools. The two that we got into were maybe 100 degrees and 96 degrees. When we ventured down into the second pool we were joined by a couple and an old guy who reeeeeally liked to hear himself talk. We walked to the 173 highway where we were to meet Marshall to take us to Arrowhead. There was a trail angel named Coppertone there who gave us root beer floats and a place to sit in the shade. Marshall took the wrong route so we hung out with Coppertone for three plus hours. Once we got to Arrowhead, Jenny and I caught some of a John Denver cover band and got a beer flight and appetizers at a place called the Grapevine in Arrowhead Village. It was awesome to go on a date again. Hiking in the mountains of my youth has also been memorable, though I did not realize that most of these mountains were desert.

DAY 25 AND 26

Zero days in Lake Arrowhead. Quality time spent with Jenny, my parents, Eddie, Luke, and Eddie and Luke's mom Margo. Finally I can repay Margo for some of the generosity that she and her family have shown me throughout the years. Saturday we went to the dock and drank beer, and ate popsicles and watermelon. It was a little surreal taking Eddie to the cabin because I mostly have memories of high school friends there. We ate stuffed cabbage and lasagna and omelettes and we went to Papagayos after Mass on Sunday. We lazed around after Papagayos and watched the Perfect Storm after dinner. Really random.

DAY 27

We said goodbye to Jenny and co. and got a late start. We decided to slackpack today because Marshall was supposed to join us but could not because he forgot his knee brace and had to wait for an Amazon delivery. We planned to do 24 miles with halfpacks on but our best laid plans were foiled. Mom and Marshall were to meet us with the rest of our packs at mile 338 but the adjacent highway was closed so they could not get to us. So we had to nighthike a few more miles until we got to Cajon Pass. Absolutely exhausted but we get to stay in the Cajon Pass Best Western on mom's dime. I finished *The Road* by Cormac McCarthy and I cried for a whole 2 miles after finishing it. Truly a low point in my trail experience. We saw two toads on the trail during the nighthike. 28 trail miles overall. That's more than one percent of the trail in one day!

DAY 28

I woke with a sore throat and a throbbing left achilles. It took me twice as long to walk the 2 blocks to McDonald's as Eddie. I suspect both my ailments are dehydration related. Given my ailments and that both Eddie and I left things in Marshall's car after stumbling deliriously into it after the night hike yesterday (I left my wallet and Eddie left his pants and one sandal) we decided to spend another zero day in Cajon Pass. Eddie was ready to go on but I thought it unwise. I will spend today on Nyquil to try and get better.

DAY 29

Today was a climbing day. Coming out of Cajon Pass and up into the Angeles National Forest. Marshall joined us today. He is slower than us but takes shorter breaks so he can keep up. Sort of boring day today. We misjudged water a little so I yogi'ed some off of a Texan guy with a truck.

DAY 30

One month on the trail. We will hike to the base of Mount Baden-Powell today. I organized for my brother Roger to pick us up tomorrow from mile 390 and take us to Burbank. It will be nice to spend time with Roger, Liesl, Sierra and Issie! Still have nagging sore throat, I hope I don't get anyone sick. Achilles was fixed with Cajon rest and witchcraft tape.

DAY 31

We started the morning by climbing a mountain. Mount Baden-Powell was 9,399 ft of elevation and took a Herculean effort to get to the top. Once at the top we did handstands and met a weird tattooed guy named Shadow. We spent the rest of the day hiking to our meeting spot with Roger. Roger picked us up and took us to In n Out. It was during this time that my stomach troubles began. I suspect Little Jim Spring to be the culprit as I was peer-pressured into not filtering the water there.

DAY 32

Sick with a stomach ailment in Burbank for our zero day. Liesl made me some weird Chinese medicines that made me feel marginally better.

DAY 33

All the way driving up to the trail I was 50-50 of starting the trail again or taking another zero at Roger's because of my stomach. I decided to tough it out because the fresh mountain air felt good. Even so I was very low energy on the trail today and we only did 13 miles.

DAY 34

Low point today for the trail for me. It is damn hot during the day. All day I was retching due to an unknown reason, perhaps because it was dusty. Nothing seemed like a good idea to eat and I was constantly needing water. SO MANY FRICKING BUGS FLIES BEES UGH

DAY 35

We woke up and hiked to the Acton KOA (Kampground of America). We are finally out of the San Gabriels. First thing I did was jump in the pool and then order a pizza. They have a convenience store here with ridiculously expensive drinks. Being a thirsty captive audience, I spent $17 on a lemonade, a milk, a naked juice, a water, and 2 cranberry juices. I went to sleep feeling much better than yesterday.

DAY 36

That didn't last long. I started feeling sick to my stomach around midnight and that's when the trains started. For some ill-begotten reason this Kampground is situated between a busy road and an obnoxiously loud train track. Nobody could get any sleep and they should relocate. Too bad they sunk all that cash into that awesome pool. Anyways, I felt absolutely awful in the morning and Eddie and Marshall hiked on without me. I ubered the ten miles to Hiker Heaven in Agua Dulce and I now think that I may have figured out the cause of my stomach trouble. Being dehydrated, I developed retching fits whenever I smelt my trail food. This made me not eat as much. When I vomited in the middle of the night there was nothing in my stomach at all even though I ate 5 pieces of pizza just a couple hours earlier. I've resolved to carry more water and different foods and hopefully I will feel better. Been a string of bad days and I am hoping the following days are better.

DAY 37

We got out of Hiker Heaven and ate breakfast at the Sweetwater Bar & Grill. I had the Bacon and Eggs with an extra side of biscuits and gravy. I felt awesome today and crushed the 17 miles. I made sure to hydrate and nutrition properly. After more thought I have concluded that I suffered from heat exhaustion the past few days. The excessive sweating, nausea, retching, and vomiting all match heat exhaustion symptoms. Tomorrow we are going to experiment with night hiking by hiking 6 miles to Casa De Luna, sleeping during the day, and starting to hike again around 7 pm. This is to avoid the excessive heat forecasted tomorrow.

DAY 38

We hiked the 6 miles to Green Valley without incident and easily got a hitch to Heart N Soul Cafe. Wonderful food at wonderful prices. I ordered my favorite breakfast plate (bacon, over-easy eggs, hash browns, and toast) with a milk. It was so good and cheap (8 bucks!) that I ordered a tuna melt and fries right afterwards. From there we walked to Casa De Luna, a hiker oasis run by a trail angel family. There we tried to nap and rest up for our night hike. After not falling asleep we played a rousing and nailbiting game of cornhole with a redhead Georgian named King Louie and a tall blond Australian named Waterboy. Terrie Anderson is such a sweet lady. She fed us dinner (nachos!) and gave us

PCT class of 2018 bandannas. We had to dance to *Uptown Funk* by Bruno Mars to get our bandanna. We set off after dinner for our night hike. After a little trouble hitching to the trail we found a ride in the back of a pick-up with a pizza delivery boy. Night hikes are spooky and mentally taxing. I listened to the Old Testament (Exodus and Leviticus) to keep my mind off things and was grateful that my headlamp worked and I had a hiking partner to walk with. Marshall is still slow so he had to walk by himself.

DAY 39

We did 12.8 of the 15 miles we wanted to nighthike because we got sleepy. Right now I am wasting away the oppressively hot daylight hours writing in my tent and listening to the incessant drone of the millions of insects outside. We are nighthiking again tonight and will hit the 500 mile mark!

DAY 40

We had a water emergency on our night hike. The water source we had rationed our water for was completely dry or else we couldn't find it during the night. We had to scoop water from the bottom of a cistern with dead snakes in it. I was completely terrified when a wild animal jumped right in front of us and scurried down the trail. I only got a glimpse of the back of it in the dark and I think it was a skunk. We're lucky it didn't spray us, but we probably already smell like hell. We hiked 10 miles til 1 AM and then started going so slow (about 1 mph) that we thought we should camp and take a nap from 1 AM to 5 AM. I've never slept better on the trail. I was so tired that I slept the four hours straight. Four hours of uninterrupted sleep is unheard of for me on this trail. Then we hiked the other 18 miles into Hiker Town. Our night hike was less successful than we had hoped, but we may have stumbled on a winning formula. 28 miles in 20 hours! Our personal record with full packs and we felt great while hiking the last 18. Hiker Town is a welcome respite from the 95+ degree heat, but it has an odd feel about it. Feels like a weird community you might find as zombie holdouts in *The Walking Dead*. We went to Neenach Cafe and had enormous Double bacon burgers and I had a mango smoothie.

DAY 41

Last night we stayed in our $10 room and you definitely get what you pay for. I had a hard futon to sleep on and there were bugs flying into me as I tried to sleep. I got so frustrated with the bugs that I pitched my tent on top of my futon as a big makeshift bug net. We will do laundry and leave Hiker Town around 5 PM to escape most of the day's heat.

DAY 42

We left Hikertown and started the infamous aqueduct stretch in the desert. Extremely picturesque and very pleasant walking in the early dusk. Truly a unique experience to be walking on top of the explanation of Los Angeles' desertly subsistence. Reading *Cadillac Desert* during this stretch is very apropos and enlightening. I also had another first tonight: cowboy camping. I have an annoying innate anxiety for bug encounters so cowboy camping is not very fun for me. It was, however, an experience that I could not pass up to cowboy camp on top of the aqueduct.

DAY 43

Was able to get maybe an hour total of sleep, and then set off right into the second half of the aqueduct stretch. Pretty uneventful day besides walking directly beneath and in between wind energy mills. Looking forward to Tehachapi arrival tomorrow night.

DAY 44

We hiked without incident to Tehachapi Willow Springs Road where Uncle David was there to pick us up and take us into town. He also took a Danish journalist named Sarah into town with us. We got to the house and Aunt Brenda made us grilled ham and cheese sandwiches. Soon, Billy Joe came home from his job at the prison and we jammed to him and Eddie's dueling guitars. After a relaxing hot tub dip, John and my parents arrived.

DAY 45

Zero day in Tehachapi. This day was spent resupplying and watching Marvel movies with our feet up. It was nice to spend time with John, David Marion, Uncle David, Aunt Brenda, and my parents. We had a father's day lunch at a BBQ place in town. I ordered the ribs but my stomach problems returned for a short period. Mary came home late that night, it was nice to see her briefly.

DAY 46

John's first day hiking with us. In retrospect it was probably unwise to have him go at our same pace. We got to camp at night and were informed that there was a bear sighting about 50 yards downhill from our campsite near the water source below. A girl ran up to us and showed us a picture of the bear she had just seen. So, we hung our food in a tree and hoped for no bearly visits that night.

DAY 47

No bear visit! John is sore and should be. His first day was 17 miles and today was 19 miles, giving him a total of 36 miles in his first two days. Comparatively, Eddie and I hiked 20 in *our* first two. We camped at Robin Bird Spring.

DAY 48

We decided to end John's misery and get him some zero days while we hiked on. We contacted Mary and asked her to pick him up. It was too big a temptation to not have Mary drive us to Lake Isabella to hit up a motel.

DAY 49

Marshall wanted to do the 5:15 AM bus while Ed and I wanted to sleep longer in the comfy beds. We got up pretty late and decided we may as well eat breakfast at a cafe because it was already late. We got our usuals, I the Bacon and eggs, and he the chicken fried steak. After that we tried to hitch to Walker Pass, but had no luck for a whole hour. We even turned to busking with our thumbs out and Ed's guitar, but still no luck. We gave up and settled for the 12:40 bus towards Walker Pass. Being so late, we only managed 12 miles though most of that was uphill.

DAY 50

Did 19 hard miles today. We saw ptarmigan/pheasant like birds that I had never seen before. The last 2.3 miles were straight uphill and I was completely drenched with sweat by the time I got to the top. Being that the sun was setting, I took the excessive sweating to mean that I was on the cusp of dehydration. Having experienced dehydration and heat exhaustion a few weeks earlier, I made sure to drink many liters of water from the stream next to our campsite before bed though I would invariably and annoyingly need to pee a couple times during the night.

DAY 51

Today we arrived at Kennedy Meadows. On the 19 mile trek in I came about 6 inches from stepping right on a rattlesnake. Startling to say the least. Today was also our first river sighting. The Kern River was cool, refreshing, and perfectly satisfying as we got there around 2 PM, the hottest part of the day. We jumped in and enjoyed the manliness of bathing in rivers. As we arrived in Kennedy Meadows we got a hitch in to Grumpy Bears where we ate double cheeseburgers and had a couple beers. Billy Joe drove John out to meet us and he definitely brings out the socialness in me somehow. Grumpy's was dingy and dirty, but it was just fine for us hiker trash.

DAY 52

We woke up and were treated to a pancake breakfast at Grumpy's. Pretty good although the potatoes were just cut up french fries. We then did our chores, took a shower, and I did some major gear overhauls at the outfitter there. I finally bought a Z pad mattress, gaiters, a titanium spoon, and a Sawyer Squeeze water filter. We had another double cheeseburger for lunch and were on our way by 3 PM. We hiked 8 miles and it looks like Eddie and John want to make a fire. I am bummed that there is no phone service out here and I can't talk with Jenny more than my generic GPS OK signal. I forgot to text her before I left Grumpy Bear WIFI because shuttle took me by surprise :(Off to Mount Whitney!

DAY 53

We lunched at an awesome river and finally got out of the damn desert! We camped and had another campfire. We were joined by a gregarious Mancunian chap and had a nice conversation. John was peddling monetary favors in exchange for labor to no success. I suspect John to be a big fat poophead. Only time will tell.

DAY 54

Suspicions confirmed. He again attempted to pawn off his daily chores like an ill-conceited miscreant. We passed by Owens valley and it was dope. We are only doing 13-14 mile days so John can keep up. Sorely missing cell service, and I fear we will be doing so until we summit Whitney in 3 days.

DAY 55

Today was a pretty easy hike, only 12.5 miles. We ended up at a gorgeous alpine lake called Chicken Spring Lake. Really feel like we've entered the High Sierras now. It is a weird feeling not having any cell phone service for 3 days straight now, this is the longest I've ever been disconnected to the world. It's disconcerting to be possibly missing some national or personal tragedy. I guess I will find out if I missed anything important when we get cell service on Mt. Whitney Summit.

DAY 56

We did a 16 mile day today with the end destination being Crabtree Meadows ranger station. We weren't allowed to have a campfire. We also had to ford a couple rivers today. A little sketchy but everyone made it across mostly unwetted. Both Marshall and I stepped on a log that looked falsely secure and got one of our feet soaked. Before this trip I would've thought that I'd need to take my shoe off and replace my drenched sock, but I've learned to just keep on walking and to only change my socks when I feel a blister hot spot forming. The major bummer of today happened a couple minutes into the day's hike. I stubbed my left big toe 3 times in a row and it finally was injured. Hurts when it flexes both up or down, so pretty much every single step. John was able to MacGyver a KT tape splint though and the pain was lessened. Concerned about how Whitney will go tomorrow.

DAY 57

I spent last night freezing my ass off and thinking about what I would do if my toe is actually a serious injury, and I'd need to quit the trail. These were some pretty intense darkies. I couldn't sleep because it was so cold, and I found myself secretly hoping that the injury is serious. I'm tired of being so tired, but the only way I'll quit is if my body physically doesn't let me hike. I put on all of my clothes that didn't reek after hiking for 5 days straight (two pairs of socks, long underwear, normal underwear gym shorts, red under armour t-shirt, REI fleece, rain jacket, neck gaiter, and beanie). I was wishing that I had a down jacket, but I hadn't needed one at all up to this point. I woke up to a world coated in frost. Today was some hardcore hiking, the hardest hiking day of the trip so far. It was only about 18 miles but the 4,000 feet elevation gain and the 6,000 feet elevation loss was killer. But I can cross Mt. Whitney summit off the bucket list! Unbelievable views though I think I was a little too tired to fully enjoy them. Eddie didn't want to carry his guitar up to the top from the junction, so I did it for him and we sang *Big Rock Candy Mountain* at the summit. When we went back to the junction we found a marmot had unzipped Eddie's pack and chewed into a bag of trail mix. Whitney Portal trail was brutal with a ridiculous amount of knee-crunching stepdowns. My trekking pole broke. My toe held up better than I had feared and I'm thinking it isn't a serious injury. This was the only day that I didn't listen to audiobooks, as I wanted to focus on the scenery and my own safety without focusing on any books as well. I have finished 22 books so far and weighed in at 206 pounds, lost 35 pounds total! When we got to Whitney Portal we had double bacon cheeseburgers and milk and juice while we waited for Marshall and John to catch up. We got a ride with an old airline vet named Kurt to our hostel in Lone Pine. Finally civilization! We will be driving through Death Valley on our way to Las Vegas to catch our flights to Seattle. The next journal day entry will be in 10 days when we get back on trail. Will be on a trail hiatus while we attend Jimmy's wedding and we spend some time with Jenny and other loved ones. It's been awesome bro time with John but he is leaving for Germany tomorrow. Everything went pretty well for how uncertainly things were planned a few months ago. I'm not sure when I'll see John next unfortunately. Marshall will be hiking ahead of us this week so we probably won't catch up to him for a month once we get back on trail.

DAY 58

10 days later. We took the 6 AM flight from Seattle to Las Vegas and were picked up by our old college buddy Chris Walsh, AKA Suga C Dubb AKA bad boy engineer. He was an engineer with us at GU and we also studied abroad in Florence with him. He acted a complete trail angel today and drove us 4.5 hours to Kearsarge Pass just outside Independence. The road trip was very enjoyable as we stopped to sightsee in Death Valley. Once at Kearsarge, there is about 7 miles of uphill hiking to get back ontrail. After 10 days offtrail I've gained back 10 of the 35 pounds I've lost. Accordingly, the hiking is tough right now, and we are also carrying 6 plus days of heavy food in our bear cans. I made a promise to Jenny that I would FaceTime her on her Birthday and so we are trying to make it to Mammoth in 6 days. Our drive with Chris went overtime so we did not get

a good start. Only 2 miles today and that puts us behind pace already.

DAY 59

Tough hiking today as the Sierra prove to be incredibly steep and stair-intensive. We again missed our goal today, falling 4 miles short of the 20 we had envisioned at the start of the day. On the bright side, the scenery is breathtaking, absolutely gorgeous. We had lunch next to upper Rae Lake and lingered too long for 2 hours. The water was crisp and refreshing.

DAY 60

Woke up early as I had a #2 emergency and quickly had to stumble out of my tent and barely eluded messing my pants. As I was going, a buck with big antlers sauntered past. First buck I've seen yet, though I see does all the time. We crossed a rickety suspension bridge that reminded me of Indiana Jones. We again ended up 4 miles shy of our 20 mile goal. I am losing hope of being in cell reception in Mammoth for Jenny's birthday. I hate breaking promises. On the bright side, our campsite is 360 degree beauty. Tomorrow looks like it will be a little easier, good because I am pooped and still wanting to hit the 20 mile mark.

DAY 61

It's the 4th of July today! The last 3-4 4th of July's I've spent at Eddie's family's cabin. Eddie tells me this is the first time in his life that he hasn't spent the 4th at his family's cabin over on Samish Island. We usually do very American things there but I think we rival the usual eat-a-lot-and-blow-things-up celebration by living off of the American wilderness. We are thinking of stopping by Vermillion Valley Resort instead of hiking straight to Mammoth like we previously planned because we are about 10 miles behind the pace needed to get to Mammoth by Jenny's birthday.

DAY 62

This is the day we summit Muir Pass, supposedly the hardest pass on the PCT usually due to lingering snow. This year, however, is a very low snow year luckily. We got to the top with no problem and there was a very cool shelter up there. About an hour later, we stopped to have lunch next to a frigid alpine lake. It was sunny and mostly windless so we decided to take a dip. Eddie noticed that it was pretty deep and so did a shallow dive as I filmed. It was like taking an ice bath, just shockingly cold. As it should be, because the lakes at this altitude (12,000 feet) are ostensibly composed of water that was snow just a few hours earlier and melted, then cascaded down the mountainside to the valley, thus forming the lake. The last few days have been 8 hour hiking days and I listen to my books 95% of the time that I'm hiking. Thus, I am completing books at an alarming rate. It feels like I am accomplishing a lifetime of reading in these few months. I'm up to 26 books completed now.

DAY 63

This day started off fast as I mistakenly fell behind Eddie and then failed to notice his backpack that he placed at the side of the trail while he went to go #2. I ended up walking 5.5 miles in one go because I thought he might still be ahead of me. I was engrossed in my *Ready Player One* audiobook so didn't notice the backpack. We crushed it today, walking almost 21 miles, making 90 miles in 5 days, our PR for sure. VVR tomorrow morning and some hot food finally. Hopefully they have cell service or WiFi so I can Facetime Jenny.

DAY 64

We got to VVR and found they had no service or Wifi. Just a Windows '99 slow computer in the back of the restaurant. Jenny's bday wishes had to be via Facebook messenger. Sigh. I was absolutely exhausted all day and I let it affect my mood unfortunately. We had some truly mediocre food and watched a firecracker World cup match between Croatia and Russia that Croatia won in penalty kicks. Eddie cheered me up when we got back on the trail by bringing out his guitar. We rocked "The Roadie" by Tenacious D. Planning to nero in Mammoth in 2 days. Hopefully, I will finally have a good night's sleep on a decent mattress and some decent food.

DAY 65

Today we are trying to cut the distance to Mammoth down to 6 or 7 miles so that we can get an early nero day in Mammoth tomorrow. We plan to go out at Duck Lake trail instead of Red's Meadow because a Guthook comment said it was good. We took the junction to Duck Lake and immediately had to hike a mile straight uphill. I began doubting that guy's comment when we got to a ridge and beautiful Duck Lake was right in front of us. We camped right on the lake and it was incredible.

DAY 66

We took the rest of Duck Lake trail and eventually stumbled upon the campground and begun to start the process of getting to Mammoth Lakes and finding a hotel to finally get off our feet. Turns out the public transportation in Mammoth in the summer is excellent and we quickly found the correct trolley to get us to town. On the way we passed a lake with some campsites next to it and saw a large bear and its cub chowing down on an unfortunate family's picnic basket. It was the first bear we'd seen the whole trip and we were on a bus instead of in the wild. We found the best deal (still expensive) with a guy named Rusty at the Sierra Lodge. Two queen beds, an ice machine, a hot tub. Heaven! We did our resupply and laundry chores, took an ice bath, a hot tub dip, and went to bed.

DAY 67

We were going to Nero out today but by 9 AM it became clear that we did not want to move at all. We paid for another night and watched the France vs. Belgium World Cup games in our beds. We spent the rest of the day wallowing in sloth and recharging our batteries. We posted our "Reasons we are doing the PCT" on our social media accounts. We got so much positive feedback from friends and random people, it was really encouraging.

DAY 68

We were planning on leaving around 7 AM but again we succumbed to the fluffy call of our beds and ended up staying until 2 pm, after the England vs. Croatia World Cup game. We took public transport to Agnew Meadows and hiked 5 miles. A passing hiker warned us of thunderstorms in the forecast.

DAY 69!

Today we planned to put in a lot of miles to make up for our lazy zero and so were targeting Tuolumne Meadows 22 miles away. We were hiking up to Donohue pass when we began noticing thunder rumbles and menacing thunder clouds in the distance. We kept walking and a couple hours later were beset by a full-on thunderstorm. We took shelter in a clump of trees near Tuolumne River and started to wait it out. Suddenly, there was a bright lightning flash and the roar of thunder followed about a half second later. The lightning struck just a half mile away! It was my first time spending a thunderstorm outside and I will admit that the proximity of the lightning freaked me out. I stood up and hurled my metal hiking poles as far as I could, just in case the lightning was attracted to the metal. The hour that we spent waiting out the storm set us back on our 22 mile goal so we had to hustle to get to Tuolumne Meadows campground. We got in just as it was getting dark and were not sure where we could legally camp. This campground was full of Yosemite tourists and they were just as clueless as we were. Since it was dark, we decided to camp wherever there was a free spot. Surely it was illegal, but we were so tired and wet from the storm that we did not care.

DAY 70

We got up around 7 at our campsite, packed up quick, and went to the restaurant where I had two breakfast biscuit sandwiches and three buckwheat pancakes. 2,200 calories for 19 dollars. I also bought a cran-grape juice, a milk, and a mango smoothie. All were amazing. I am thinking of carrying a liter of cran-grape with me while I hike because it gives me such an intense spiritual boost. We then said farewell to Tuolumne and hiked 5 miles to an impressive waterfall called Tuolumne Falls. Eddie played a song called Tuolumne on his guitar that he knew from childhood. A few unfortunate things happened to me today. Firstly, my rain cover ripped as I attempted to save my backpack from getting drenched. Fortunately it still mostly works. Secondly, I lost my balance on a log in a stream and both shoes got totally soaked, compounding this was the fact that the sun was almost down. Thirdly, I stubbed my left big toe again and tried to balance myself with my poles but fell directly onto my face. My knee would have taken the brunt of the fall but I had my knee brace on and so was protected. I hadn't worn my knee braces for a couple days before then, so that was pretty lucky. We got checked by our first park ranger of the whole trip today. All compliant. Camped at beautiful Miller Lake and dried my clothes with the campfire.

DAY 71

We got a late start and hit the dusty trail. I listened to *Switch* by Dan Heath, *The Perfect Storm* by Sebastian Junger, Ezekiel from the Old Testament, and *Walden* by Henry David Thoreau. We covered Benson Pass and Sealey Pass. Tough hiking today, I had thought most of the hard Sierra was already done. Tomorrow looks tough as well. We are aiming for Kennedy Meadows North after two days hiking. My big toe joint is killing me again. My splint was less effective today and my pen is running out of ink. This thing was like 12 bucks and is supposed to be weatherproof.

DAY 72

Two days til we can hitch into Kennedy Meadows North. Today was not too eventful. We went up and down another pass and saw some horses. These were the first horses I've seen all trail though I have been dodging their poop for the last 400 miles. We got checked by another forest ranger named PJ and she said that we should have been packing out our toilet paper while in the Yosemite area. We had no idea. According to Guthook, today was supposed to be "mosquito hell" going up to Dorothy Lake pass. It actually wasn't as bad as some other parts of the Sierra though, we must have missed the big mosquito swarm. I wear long pants and long sleeve shirts, and sometimes I put a bug net over my face, and I have been wearing three different types of insect repellant

(Deet, Picaridin, and Permethrin) so the mosquitoes don't affect me too much. If insect repellant didn't exist, I would not be out here. Dorothy Lake was probably the most beautiful lake we've seen thus far. It was at the very end of the day by the time we got there so the dusklight shed a purple shadow on the mountain behind the lake. Purple mountains majesty indeed! We also heard a coyote sounding howl at one point. This was strange because we don't think there are coyotes in the Sierra, no idea what it was.

DAY 73

We get into Kennedy Meadows North today. 18 miles. Days when we hike into town always go fast because we are extra motivated to get into town and lay in bed and eat and shower. We did 18 miles by 4 PM passing amazing amazing scenery on the way. We hiked atop a mountain and took lunch when we got to the top. During the Sierra I have been extremely lax about how much water I have because there are streams every mile or two (as opposed to the desert where I was always concerned about where the next water source was). Anyways, I drank all of my water at lunch and then, to my dismay, saw on my navigation app that the next water wouldn't be for 7 miles. I geared myself up mentally to be thirsty for the next couple hours. There weren't official water sources for the next 7 miles because we were hiking along a beautiful high ridge that whole time instead of valleys and lakes. I was just getting very thirsty by the 4th mile, when I noticed a snow patch above me that had a little stream of melt coming from it. I filled my water bottle and tasted the best, coldest, water I've had in my whole life. Maybe because I was so thirsty, or because it was freshly melted snow. When we got to the Sonora Pass highway, there was trail magic! Free hot dogs and beer. We walked into Kennedy Meadows North and got steak dinners and I talked to a Hong Kong guy named Cliff for an hour about his life in Hong Kong. He told me that China has started instituting a Loyalty Points system for its citizens where a citizen can't even buy a train ticket unless they've been a good citizen (meaning they've been paying bills on time, and not being a criminal). Hit a thousand miles today!!!

DAY 74

New Pen! Kennedy Meadows North was one of Eddie's and my favorite spots. There was a good cheap restaurant that was open from 6 AM to 9 PM, a good resupply store, cheap beds, laundry, showers, and an awesome wraparound porch to hang out on. Everything a hiker could want. Seems like this pen rubs off on my hand if I'm not careful, lame. We resolved to leave Kennedy Meadows North by 12 PM but, due to their awesome restaurant, were lucky to gather enough motivation to get out the door by 5 PM. Once we finally left, we had a lot of trouble finding a hitch back to the trail. After 30 fruitless minutes of pointing our thumbs at passing cars, I decided to try my luck by perusing the nearby campsites and convincing one of the campers to take a half hour out of their day to help some poor thru-hikers get back to the trail. It takes a certain amount of gumption to work up the courage to walk up to strangers and beg for charity. The first group I tried was drunk past driving capability. The second group made an excuse that their trailer was on uneven ground and would take forever to move. As I talked to a 3rd group who was in the midst of turning me down, a guy name Rich from the 2nd group approached me and said he had a change of heart and that his trailer tilt wasn't actually that bad. Hitch secured! Though I'm not sure what changed his mind. He drove Eddie, myself, and a German older woman named Early Bird back to the trail and exhorted us to take pulls from a bottle of Jack Daniels whiskey he had in his glove compartment. It would have been rude to turn down this generosity. Once on trail, we did a few more miles and hunkered down for the night.

DAY 75

We were feeling ambitious after our KM nero, and decided to do a 23 mile day, one of the biggest days on trail yet. I broke the 8 hour audiobook listening barrier that I had been flirting with for weeks, falling just a few minutes short more than a couple times. We ended the day camping at the saddle above Noble Lake. I was entertained by Don Quixote's hilarious miscues on the climb up to the saddle, laughing audibly to myself several times.

DAY 76

I slipped on a 45 degree slope and smacked my face with my hiking pole while trying to regain my balance. I was surprised that I didn't give myself another bloody nose. The day before getting into town is always the hardest. Town is so close, yet so far, and you can't start to loaf or else you won't be able to get to town the next day. Looking forward to Tahoe and spending time with my godfather and his wife.

DAY 77

We hiked the last few miles to the pass and were surprised by the generosity of everyone in the area. We were greeted at the visitor center with a cold Pepsi and a box of glazed donuts. One lady even stopped us and handed us each $40, saying she always wanted to hike the trail and that we are hiking it for her. Unbelievable. I finally have some income from this trip! We had to take 3 different hitches to get to South Lake Tahoe but we finally got to our meeting place we arranged with my godfather, an all-you-can-eat sushi joint called Sato. On the trail, you mostly eat your camp food, or at a burger joint in whatever small town you wander into. Lake Tahoe boasts many different cuisines and we were going to take advantage of that, hence the several tons of sushi we shoveled down. I weighed myself at the visitor's center and was shocked to see that I weighed 191 pounds, 50 pounds less than when I started the trail. I doubted the scale but was assured by the volunteers that it was correct. Can't believe I've lost that much.

DAY 78

My godfather's house was fantastic. I had my own bedroom and bathroom for the first time this whole trip. I spent my time lounging in the queen bed and eating ripe peaches.

DAY 79

My godfather and his wife drove us back to the trailhead. We thanked them profusely and enjoyed leftover tri-tip sandwiches for our first couple meals. I love listening to a new audiobook and finding that it references or quotes a different book that I have just read on this trip. This happened when Michael Pollan quoted Walden in his *The Omnivore's Dilemma*. It makes me feel very in-the-know. We keep passing tall trees with intensely green moss on them. The moss invariably starts growing on the trunks about 15 feet off the ground, regardless of the elevation the tree is itself at. A wonder of biological nature.

DAY 80

It is on this day that I first began thinking of writing a book of my own after I am finished with the trail. While listening to *Crushing It* by Gary Vaynerchuk, one of the chapters regards a guy who helps people pass LEED green exams for the construction business. He has a website and makes a modest income but soon decides to sell an e-book on his website that pretty much summarizes the site. He thus begins to acquire passive income from the sales of his books. He wakes up the next morning and finds that he's sold a couple books and is a little richer. This story, combined with the 10 odd other business books that I've read now gets me thinking about how the structure of all of these business books is more or less formulaic and copiable. They usually consist of about 3 or so total hours of original, interesting thought by the author sandwiched between about 5 or so total hours of interesting historical anecdotes that back up their hypotheses. It has struck me that I could do the same thing with my business idea. Armed with the 3ish hours of original thought already, all I need to do is research some historical anecdotes that support. I already know of Frank Lloyd Wright and myself that have benefitted from Absorbent Learning. Heck, I'm auditorily Absorbent Learning on this whole trip and only started hatching this plan because I am doing so. The last chapter could be a biographical account of this trip. I am thus inspired to read a Frank Lloyd Wright biography and to read some how-to books about writing and publishing original works. Besides this revelation, today was full of interesting sights. We passed through 3 ski resorts. Alpine Meadows, Squaw Valley, and Sugar Bowl. We also walked through the infamous Donner Pass, where the snowed-in and desperate Donner Party of the late 1800s allegedly resorted to cannibalism to stay alive on their way to California. I remember learning about them in 6th grade social studies class. It's weird what the mind chooses to recollect when I can scarcely remember anything else from the whole 6th grade. Instead of eating other hikers, we dined on nachos and western cheeseburgers from the ski ranch in the Donner Valley.

DAY 81

We started heading towards Sierra City. About ¾ through the day we rethought our conviction to stay at Sierra City, now intending to stay in the town of Quincy, about 40 miles further on. This decision was made chiefly because of negative Guthook comments about Sierra City and positive guthook comments about Quincy. Also, we have a surplus of food that can last us another couple days anyhow. We are coming up on mile 1200 in the next couple miles.

DAY 82

We got a great start and we actually made the 23 miles to the Sierra City junction before 5 PM. So we did another about face and decided to go into Sierra City after all, but just for the night. We had carnitas burritos and lemonade for dinner. Lemonade after a 23 mile hike is heavenly. To save money, we slept in a generous Methodist church parking lot. There was a cold shower in a public restroom nearby that we gratefully used.

DAY 83

The next day I woke up to find my sunglasses snapped at both hinges. Somehow the weight displaced something in my bag and crushed them. I bought them for 30 bucks at a golf course last year and was surprised they lasted 82 trail days. I threw them away and resolved to find some in the tiny town of Sierra City. We had cottage cheese and bacon for breakfast and after a few minutes of searching, I checked off every place in town that could conceivably sell sunglasses. There were no sunglasses for sale in the entire town! So, I completed my evolution into a true homeless vagrant and went to the trash can that I threw my broken sunglasses into and fished them out. After fixing them as best I could with duct tape, I went and washed my hands. We took an alternate route up some dirt roads to get back to the trail. 13 miles of hills today.

DAY 84

My repaired sunglasses don't stay on my face but slide down my nose when I begin to sweat. Consequently, every hill we climb I have to reach up and poke my sunglasses back up to the bridge of my nose every minute or so. Very bright the last couple days. We have been keeping pace with a motley group of hikers since Donner Pass. There's a small fiery dude named Jackrabbit. There's a guy named Danny Boy that seems miserable on trail but when you hand him a beer he lights up and turns into his buzzed alter ego named "Uncle Baby." There's 3 Japanese hikers that have the thickest accents I've ever heard. Lastly, there's an old warrior of a woman named Mosey who must be at least 65 years old. She hikes faster than us most of the time.

DAY 85

We aimed for the highway and did the 22 miles by 6 PM. When we got there, we tried to hitch into Quincy but struck out for a half hour. While we were there, the rest of the hiking group showed up and a trail angel named Chuck arrived at the perfect time with a 30 rack of Natty Ice and an 18 pack of root beer. We enjoyed each other's company for about an hour and Eddie and I camped on the side of the road and will try to hitch into Quincy tomorrow morning.

DAY 86

This is the least traveled paved road that I've ever seen. Including last night we've seen 3 cars pass by. Writing my diary as I sit on the side of the road while Eddie is playing Led Zeppelin on his guitar… 4 hours later and still nobody stopping for a hitch. Not a lot of traffic on this road but I am beginning to suspect that our beards deter would-be stoppers. Finally we got a hitch from a guy named Riley who was doing a post-graduation road trip. We got into Quincy and Riley dropped us off at the Spanish Creek Motel. We said goodbye to Riley, turned around, and saw Marshall sitting on a bench. Completely unplanned. We walked to Round Table Pizza because we heard about there being an all you can eat pizza buffet. When we got there we found that the all you can eat deal was for weekdays only and today is Saturday. Boo! We resupplied and spent the rest of our day relaxing and doing our laundry in our bathroom sink because the only laundromat in town was 3 stinkin miles away.

DAY 87

As usual, we talked about leaving town after breakfast at eleven but stayed until after lunch instead. For both meals we went to a restaurant called Morning Thunder. Hefty portions. We hiked 7 miles after getting a hitch immediately (our last hitch was 7 hours, this one was 5 minutes). We camped with a hiker named Starburst who says that a mountain lion has been terrorizing her for the last week. It's been outside her tent and she's heard it screaming in heat. We have yet to see a mountain lion and I'm glad not to see one.

DAY 88

Interesting day as we hiked down a huge 8 mile hill to the river town of Belden and then hiked back up a 5 mile hill afterwards. Belden was just finishing up a music festival when we arrived and the town was full of electronica gypsies packing up their tents and leaving. Lots of very dirty hippies. We hung out with some hikers by the roaring Feather River. Wreck-it (a 3 star Michelin Chef), Uncle Baby, Starburst, a German, and a couple Israelis rounded out the group. After a couple beers, the ensuing hill hike was much harder.

DAY 89

We had to do the rest of that huge hill coming out of Belden today. The good news is that the trail is relatively flat for the next 700 miles as we finish up Northern California and Oregon. Once we get into the Washington Cascades, the steep hills will be back with vengeance. The hill took half the day and we ended up camping at Robber Creek. We will reach the halfway point of the PCT tomorrow! Will end the day in Chester.

DAY 90

The days that I hike into town are always the worst. The miles go by in slow motion while my cravings for food and everything else societal are ratcheted into high gear. Even the midpoint monolith failed to excite me as all I wanted to do was get to town and lay on a bed. Halfway done though and it's all downhill from here metaphorically. When we got into town I was bitterly disappointed to find every motel booked and we would have to camp in the backyard of a Lutheran Church. I bought a large milkshake to cheer myself up and it worked. I will be going offtrail tomorrow to see Jenny at my friend Nick's wedding in Portland. Excited for this! Marshall and Eddie will hike on without me and I will meet them in 3 days. My lower back has been bothering me, I suspect my cumbersome bearcan to be the culprit.

Four Days Later…

DAY 95

Eddie and Marshall had done two 30-mile days prior to meeting me at Burney Mountain Guest Ranch and so wanted to take a nero out. This place was awesome. We were treated to breakfast burritos and waffles for breakfast. There was a stand-up player piano and a guitar that Eddie and I jammed on. We jumped in the pool, hung out on the porch, and drank chocolate milk. We hiked 9 miles and stayed at Burney Falls Park.

DAY 96

We camped in the state park and set off for the day's hike. We passed a few hikers that were trying to hitch into Mt. Shasta and skip this 90 mile section because they thought the recent California wildfires have made the trail too smoky to hike. The smoke is definitely a visible shroud, but I can't even smell it. I forget who said it, but I read a quote recently that said it is a uniquely human trait to be able to rationalize almost anything. These people have reasoned that skipping is the best move and so they are doing it. Why should I care? It's their hike. We passed the beautiful Burney Falls waterfall and hiked on towards Mt. Shasta.

DAY 97

Today was my first 30 mile day! We were ambitious about our mileage because we saw that the elevation profile was mostly flat or downhill. It was a long day and very humid and smoky. I finished three of my books today (*Don Quixote*, a writing book, and the *Quran*). I am strangely sad that I'm done with Quixote. Although the first half was much better than the second half, I enjoyed the narrator's portrayal of Quixote and Sancho. I finished my 30 miles at about 8:30 PM and had just enough daylight to filter some water from the McCloud River. I set up camp and ate two packets of freeze-dried Spanish Rice in the dark. Will be sore tomorrow, but I've been working up to a 30 mile day on this whole trip and I feel badass!

DAY 98

Today was the worst smoke so far. I could smell it and was noticeably uncomfortable. I used my respirator but the strap broke later in the day, will need to get a new one in Shasta tomorrow. We jumped in a creek and took some pretty cool pictures under a bridge. Eddie found a deep spot and did a dive that I would consider foolishly dangerous. That's the difference between me and Ed. Marshall said he saw a mama black bear and two cubs. When he startled them, the two cubs clambered swiftly up a nearby tree. At the end of the day, we ran into a hiker that we met on the first day of our trip back in Mexico named Kathleen. My parents and her parents actually met when they dropped us off. She said her entire "trail family" of six all had to quit the trail and now she had to walk by herself. She is going to drive through Oregon once she gets to Shasta. We will be in Shasta tomorrow morning! Food food food food food…

DAY 99

We reached the 5 freeway. I've been here before on driving trips to Seattle. We got a hitch from a nondescript guy named Ken. Ken took us to the Black Bear Diner and I ate a 3,000 calorie breakfast that consisted of chicken fried steak, biscuits, potatoes, 3 over-easy eggs, a vanilla malt, and way too much gravy. I had an upset stomach for the rest of the day and had to hit the restroom 4 times. We did our chores, I bought a new respirator, Ed bought new shoes, and Marshall bought a hideous new booger-green hiking shirt. We checked into the Alpine Inn and went to a place called Mike and Tony's for dinner. We had carbonara and delicious soup and salad and a bottle of cab sav to celebrate 1500 miles finished! I facetimed Jenny for an hour or so and then we vegetated on our motel beds and watched *Harry Potter and the Goblet of Fire* on the TV.

DAY 100

We are going to nero out of Shasta today. As of now we are being ambitious and attempting the next 150 mile section to Seiad Valley in 6 days. We bought six days worth of food but the challenge will be stretching my cell phone battery out for 6 days while listening incessantly to my audiobooks during my hiking. We'll see how much I can conserve battery. We went back to the Black Bear Diner for lunch and I got a mushroom swiss cheeseburger and a huckleberry milkshake. We got a ride from an ex-highway patrol guy named Tony back to the trail. We hiked 13 miles uphill to a campsite surrounded by very tall trees swaying in the light breeze. As we were setting up camp, we heard a loud boom from somewhere nearby. I had no idea what it was but Marshall quickly identified it as a widowmaker AKA a tree falling and crashing to the ground. The rest of the night I was somewhat anxious as I watched the trees swaying around my tentsite.

DAY 101

We tried to do 29 miles today but only made it 28 before it got dark, so close… We probably didn't make it on account of the long break we took at the beautiful Porcupine Lake. I didn't see any porcupines but I did see a frog when I dipped my feet in.

DAY 102

We decided to call an audible and hitch into Etna instead of hiking straight to Seiad Valley. This turned out to be an awesome decision for a few reasons. 1) The bunkhouse we stayed at was amazing and 2) Marshall came down with a stomach sickness. The bunkhouse was essentially someone's backyard/garage area. Normally we would pay $70 a night to stay somewhere in town but at this place the host only asked that we do some chores around the house. We were told to weed a small portion of her garden which we'll do tomorrow morning. What a deal! We spent the night jamming and having fun with some other hikers named Rocket, Captain, Thad, and E.T. Was really fun.

DAY 103

The other hikers left for the trail but we resolved to take a zero because we liked Etna so much. We got breakfast where Eddie had a chicken fried steak that he rated a dismal 1.7 out of 10. My bacon and eggs were superb. To save money we are cooking our own dinner tonight with the BBQ at the bunkhouse. Sirloins with a potato/pepper/onion/mushroom scramble on the side. 17 dollars total. Marshall is struggling with a diarrhea sickness, but Eddie and I feel fine. We did our chores, and Eddie played Guitar Hero 3 with the Wii.

DAY 104

Sad to leave Etna but the trail beckons. Marshall has to stay behind because of his sickness. We got breakfast burritos and hitched out of town with a grandpa named Peter who said that he hadn't done a good deed today yet so he thought he should pick us up. Nice guy. We got to the trailhead and hiked to a small lake where Eddie tried to fish with the rod he carries. No luck… this is only the third time on the whole trip that he's tried fishing. His backpack is probably 20 pounds heavier than mine, and he hikes without hiking poles, and it's all I can do to keep up with him. We kept hiking for 4 miles after the lake and it was a very eventful 4 miles! I saw my first bear cub in the wild. I had seen some bears from a bus when I was in Mammoth, but this one I saw while I was hiking. I was walking along a ravine side and saw him running away from me on the other side of the ravine. Black bear. We then hit a pass in the mountain and coming out the other side there was some beautiful alpine lake scenery and one of the most beautiful sunsets I've ever seen. The smoke in the distance made the sun change colors from pink to red to orange then back to red. The orange was so orange that I started craving orange juice! That night we set up camp and as soon as it got dark, we heard VERY loud footsteps running past our camp. I couldn't see anything because my rain fly was up but Eddie thought it was for sure the mama bear. I went to sleep more easily than I probably should have, but Eddie said he heard the bear rushing back to return from wherever it went at about 5 in the morning. I was fast asleep.

DAY 105

The next day we hiked 25 miles toward Seiad Valley. I got stung by something a couple hours into the day. This was my first sting for the whole hike, I was beginning to think I was unattractive. Whatever it was stung me through my hiking pants on the inside of my left thigh about halfway between my knee and my groin. It's very itchy and is swollen. We camped at Grider Creek.

DAY 106

Today we got up very early so that we could hike the 12 miles into Seiad Valley and get in in time before the Cafe there stopped serving breakfast. We had read about the famous Seiad Valley Pancake challenge for the last couple weeks and were excited to give it a go. We even made a side wager between us that whoever ate less had to pay for the whole meal. The challenge is to eat five 1 pound pancakes within 2 hours. The pancakes were humongous and we only managed to eat 51% for me and 48% for Eddie. I was victorious! Seiad Valley is very anti-California and they have signs everywhere saying they want to secede from California and create a 51st US state called Jefferson. Quite a unique place.

DAY 107

We hiked the big hill out of Seiad. After checking my Apple tracker, I realized we had done more elevation gain today than any other day on the trail. This came as a surprise to me because I didn't really feel that tired. The body has become a hardened hiking machine. We did 4,000 feet of elevation gain. My biggest annoyance nowadays is the sting that I got on my left hamstring area. It is in a location that rubs against my hiking pants and gets very aggravated as I hike. Even putting KT tape on it only provides marginal relief. I bought anti itch cream in Seiad but it is not effective. Boo! Oregon Tomorrow!!!

DAY 108

We had 12 miles to Oregon and were very motivated to get out of the huge enormous gigantic state of California. 1700 miles in a single state. Right before we got to the border we happened upon the ruins of a 1930s cabin that was recently made semi-habitable by trail angels. It was completely abandoned when we got there but there were traces of hikers spending the night. I find it weird that people would sleep there when they could walk another half mile and make it to Oregon. The border itself was just a sign in the middle of the forest. Still, it felt like the biggest milestone thus far. The only other one that may have rivaled it was when we crossed the 100 mile mark back in April. We hiked a few miles past the border but when we reached our intended campsite, it was at a very windy part of a mountain. We decided to hike a mile further to the other side of the mountain.

DAY 109

Today I woke up to a beautiful sunrise. It's not often that I camp in a spot that has an unimpeded eastern view, while also waking up early enough to see it. We made it to Ashland via hitchhike from a bartender named Zahara. Ashland is a College town known for its Shakespeare festivals. We did our laundry and got 50 cent frosties from Wendy's.

DAY 110

Zero day in Ashland. Today was spent relaxing and doing chores. I got some thank you cards from the post office and got a delicious eggs and bacon meal with crispy polenta at a fantastic brunch spot called Morning Glory. Eddie got the linguica omelette. We shopped for the rest of our food and spent the rest of the day on our backs in our comfy motel beds. We watched *Finding Nemo*, *Finding Dory*, *Ratatouille*, and *Parent Trap*. That night we went to another motel to meet up with some hikers. Their motel had a pool and a sauna, we ended up at 7/11 afterwards where I bought a big bag of corn nuts.

DAY 111

We hadn't planned on spending two zeroes in Ashland but I wanted Marshall to catch up with us. Today was even lazier than yesterday because all of our chores were already done.

DAY 112

We got breakfast at a falafel spot where the owner gave us free frozen lemonades for being hikers. A guy named Mark that sold Abalone shells for a living gave us a ride back to the trail. We hiked 16 miles and camped next to a road for the night.

DAY 113

Today we hiked 28 miles, the miles were pretty easy, Oregon is much flatter than California. The nights are getting very cold again but that has corresponded with much less smoke. I bet the fires are subsiding. Good timing because we may be able to see Crater Lake when we get there in a couple days. We have been seeing pictures of hikers where the lake is completely shrouded in smoke and they can't even see the famous island in the middle. We saw a fox today! I was turning a corner in the trail and saw it off to my right. It immediately ran away. 90% sure it was a red fox because I had heard there were some of those in Oregon. I feel lucky to have spotted one. We also went to Hyatt Lake Resort for breakfast.

DAY 114

Today we planned on hiking 28 more miles, but were delayed when we decided to go off-trail for lunch at Fish Lake Resort. We waited a half hour for a hitch in and had to walk 2 miles after failing to secure a hitch after lunch. I had a double cheeseburger with chili cheese fries and a milkshake.

DAY 115

Today was awesome if only for the fact that we were walking through a burn for most of the day. I was looking for morel mushrooms as I was walking by. In *The Omnivore's Dilemma*, Michael Pollan talks about how mushrooms like to pop up after the tree they were leeching off dies in a fire. I didn't see any unfortunately but i didn't venture too far off trail to look. We camped in a spot that didn't have any noticeable trees that were going to fall.

DAY 116

Today we hiked 10 miles into Mazama Village which is just south of Crater Lake. We took a little shortcut via a highway roadwalk. When we got in we immediately went to the restaurant where I got all-you-can-eat soup and salad. I had two large plates of salad and caught up on my veggie intake. My mom would be proud! We camped in the forest next to the showers. We went in the showers but there wasn't any soap. We played guitar at the campsite and Rocket, Freewheel, and Peach rolled in, so we jammed a little then went to bed.

DAY 117

We took the shuttle to the Rim Village at Crater Lake. Crater Lake itself was incredible. We were very lucky to be there on a day where there was no smoke. I'd say today was second only to Mt. Whitney for incredible views. We took our time on the rim and spent around 7-8 hours up there. We did 100 pushups at the top because we felt like we needed an upper body workout after all the lower body hiking workouts we've done recently.

DAY 118

Today we hiked more than any other day so far. 33 trail miles and I feel very accomplished but so tired. My left big toe injury that cropped up on Mt. Whitney came back towards the end of the day. Tomorrow will be tough if I don't splint it. We are trying to make it to Shelter Cove Resort tomorrow.

DAY 119

Today we did 27 miles and hiked into the awesome Shelter Cove. It was really hard hiking for me today because of my toe. I splinted it with KT tape, but it still was hurting. It got so bad I stopped listening to *The Gulag Archipelago* and listened to *The Long Walk* by Stephen King instead. This book is pretty messed up, true to King's normal style, but it got me interested enough to forget about my toe for a little. We were racing to get to Shelter Cove before the restaurant closed. I was the last person to get into the resort because I was slow on account of my toe. I got there ten minutes after it closed so was very disappointed until Marshall told me he ordered me a burger before it closed. I was very happy, thanks bro!

DAY 120

We woke up and got a good breakfast at the restaurant. We had originally intended on hiking out 8 miles tonight, but ended up just taking a lazy zero. Shelter Cove restaurant is really good and relatively cheap. So we did our laundry and jumped in the cold lake and air dried in the sun. I had baby-back ribs and fries for 10 dollars and we had some beers afterwards. It was fun and I definitely appreciated the zero day. We are aiming for Bend in 3 days.

DAY 121

I could tell that the rest of the group I was hiking with was lollygagging after we ate breakfast and nobody had any sense of urgency in their movements. I couldn't blame them because Shelter Cove was awesome but I need to average 21 miles per day to make it to Canada on October 7th because I have a flight to Germany to visit with John on that day. It's a hard deadline and it's a great motivator to get going. So I decided to leave before everyone in order to inspire them to get moving. Turns out that this inspiration trick worked only for Marshall as he and I camped alone that night. Eddie and the rest of the group were sucked into the comfortable vortex of Shelter Cove for a second zero day. It was the first time in the whole trip that Eddie and I camped apart, kinda weird. I spent the whole day hiking alone and it actually felt kind of liberating. I didn't have to check in with anyone and I could take breaks whenever I felt like it. Subsequently, I took twice as many breaks. We camped at Irish Lake, the water sources on this section of the trail are mostly stagnant lakes. Still hiking through forest for the most part with the occasional lake view.

DAY 122

Today was a pretty nondescript hiking day. We did 29 miles and it was mostly a green forest tunnel. I did see a very interesting bird towards midday. It was as big as a hawk and I saw it gliding down the slope from me so I could see the tops of its wings while it was gliding. On either side of his body were tufts of red plumes sticking up from each of its wings like twin cowlicks. I've never seen a bird like this and it flew by too fast to snap a picture of it. Marshall and I touched base throughout the day and camped at sister Mirror Lake at the end of the day. We could see the three Sister mountains today. We are going to stay in Sisters tomorrow night and will be getting picked up by my old roommate Matt around 7 PM because he happened to be in the area. We also hiked on and off with a German guy named Big Bro who is from Augsburg.

DAY 123

Today was a top 10 day in terms of scenery. We hiked past the beautiful Obsidian Falls and through black lava fields. There were chunks of obsidian everywhere you looked. Today was the day before a zero day though and that means it is extra difficult to walk the distance. Mentally, I was counting down the seconds for the last 7 or 8 miles. It didn't help that the last mile of the day before we got to the freeway was a lava field of sharp jagged rock. After hiking 150ish miles in the last 6 days (including a zero day) my feet were screaming indignantly at me and they especially hated this last jagged talus section. After a few minutes, Matt picked us up and treated us to a Mexican feast in the town of Sisters. I got the carne asada plate. Sisters seems to be a pretty touristy town. We skipped the motels and stayed in a Trail Angel named Prem's backyard. Matt and I had a few beers and caught up around a fireless fire pit.

DAY 124

Prem made us huckleberry pancakes and a zucchini based scramble. It was delicious. Prem's place is very rustic-modern and she has 2 cats, 1 dog, and 4 horses. Prem herself is amazingly generous, but also quite odd. She seems to believe in both astrology and karma, which I think is utter nonsense. Then again, she probably wouldn't offer us her home if she didn't believe in that stuff, so why should I judge? Marshall and I went into Bend and did our chores, said goodbye to Matt, and hung out by the Deschutes River sipping a beer from Bend Brewing Company. Prem picked us up and made us pizza at night. She also let me borrow her car to pick up Eddie who had made it to the highway we got to last night. Eddie and I used the hot tub and caught up. Prem is the best.

DAY 125

I was not going to spend 2 zeroes but the timing of the wedding I need to get offtrail for necessitates me to stay in the Bend area. If I had hiked onwards I would be in the wilderness when I needed to access public transportation.

So it looks like I will be spending six zero days in a row in order to attend a wedding in San Francisco for one of Jenny's college friends. I am going so I can spend time with Jenny. She has been a trooper for the last 4 months while I've been away. Marshall decided to hike on while Eddie and I went back to Bend so he could do his chores. We had French Toast for breakfast and said farewell to Prem. Eddie and I went to the Deschutes brewery and the 10 Barrel brewery.

DAY 126

Smoke is rolling into Bend from the new fires down in NorCal near Mt. Shasta. We have been blessed with smokeless skies for the last couple weeks and I was just beginning to take it for granted again. Today we went to a restaurant called the Breakfast Club where Eddie and I ordered our usuals: chicken fried steak and bacon and eggs respectively. I ran to the gear shop and fixed a broken zipper on my tent and jumped on the Greyhound bus to Eugene and then to Portland. I am catching up on my journal as I am riding in the bus, hence my questionable penmanship. I am looking forward to dinner tonight with Nick & Sasha and breakfast tomorrow with my parent's cousins Ray and Sandy. Ray and Sandy will take me to the airport tomorrow afternoon so I can catch my San Fran flight.

Three days later…

DAY 129

Successful wedding and great quality time with Jenny. I ubered to the San Jose airport and flew back to Portland. Ray and Sandy met me again and drove me to Government Camp where I was to meet Marshall. They treated me to a much appreciated meal.

DAY 130

Government Camp is a small town located next to the Mount Hood Ski Resort. Marshall was ill with a stomach sickness and Eddie was going to show up later in the day so I needed to take another zero. Eddie showed up and we had chicken fried steaks and burgers for dinner at the Huckleberry Inn. He says this is the best chicken fried steak he's had the entire trip.

DAY 131

I was antsy to get going so Ed and I decided to go up to Timberline Lodge. Marshall is skipping this section due to his illness. I heard him going to the bathroom 5-6 times overnight. Timberline Lodge is famous for being the hotel in the Stephen King movie *The Shining*. They are also famous for having an awesome buffet that most PCT hikers take advantage of. We had whole salads, soups, charcuterie boards, cheese boards, roast potatoes, roast beef, pork chops, and huckleberry tarts… yum!! Once we got to the Lodge it started pouring rain and we procrastinated starting to hike for as long as we could then set out through the storm. We heard it would snow that night so we decided to hike out of there and get to lower elevation and not have to deal with the snow. We made it 10 miles that night and were fortunate that the rain had stopped by the time we made camp. I was raring to go a long distance tomorrow because it had been a while since I hiked.

DAY 132

We were 40 miles from Cascade Locks and I decided to try for a PR and do the whole 40 miles in one day. Eddie didn't want to, so I got up at 4:30 AM and left him in the dust. I hiked with my headlamp for the first couple hours, but I noticed it dim considerably by the time I stopped using it. I had no extra batteries because I used my extra ones to replace my emergency gps batteries a few days ago. Everything was going fine until the rain started pouring in sheets. I threw on my big blue poncho, but there was no escaping the torrents. Though the rain made things miserable, I think it made me hike faster because I took less breaks. I needed to keep hiking to stay warm and even then I was losing feeling in my hands. I saw Washington for the first time in the distance across the river below. By the time I started the descent into Cascade Locks (about 33 miles into the day) it was starting to get dark and I was starting to get delirious. I called my dad for his birthday and took a wrong turn while I was talking to him. It took me about 0.5 miles down the wrong hill to notice. Luckily I decided to check my map somewhat soon and realized my horrible mistake. I turned around and hiked back up the hill I just came down. When I got back to the top, I had 5 miles to go and the sun had set. My headlamp was losing battery power so I had to walk with increasingly dim light. The trail was strewn with jagged talus rocks for miles at a time and with the dim light and my delirious exhausted mental state I would twist my ankle every 10 minutes and scream out loud in pain. Luckily, my ankles are complete badasses at this point of the trail, and they heal after about 20 steps. If I had twisted my ankle like that at the beginning of the trail, I would've been injured for a couple days at least. It was cold and windy and I was completely drenched as I approached Cascade Locks. About a mile and a half from town I took another demoralizing wrong turn. I couldn't see the turn in the dark and I went down another wrong hill for another half mile. I screamed as loud as I could and turned around. Finally, at 9:30 PM I hobbled under the bridge and made it to a convenience store. I sat down, drenched in the entrance, the store attendant told me he was closing in a couple minutes, so I grabbed a peach iced tea Snapple and drank it in two gulps. I limped towards Marshall's motel room, it was hard to choose which leg to favor and I ended up alternating my limp until I collapsed into Marshall's motel room, so grateful that I didn't have to set up my drenched tent. Taking the wrong turns into account I hiked 42 miles in 16 hours, definitely a personal record. I doubt the Cascades in Washington will let me hike more than 42. When I got to the motel room, I peeled off my sopping wet clothes and limped into the bathroom. I climbed into the shower and turned the shower knob. The knob wasn't labelled well because our hotel was super cheap and the water was immediately burning hot. The water scalded my skin that had been made extra sensitive by my wet clothes. It was one of the most painful experiences of my entire life. I fell to my knees and fumbled for the shower controls to turn off the hot water. I collapsed on the shower floor and laid there for a good 15 minutes with cool water running over me. I didn't have the energy to eat a meal and went straight to bed afterwards. My chafed thighs were burning in bed.

DAY 133

Zero in Cascade Locks. I could barely walk in the morning with the insides of my ankles hurting the most. I laid in bed for most of the day until Eddie got in around 4. We then met up with Eddie's Uncle Steven and Aunt Karen who made us sirloin and salmon and were great trail angels.

DAY 134

Today we would have kept hiking into Washington if it weren't for plans we made with our friend Andrei to stay at his cabin in Mt Hood back in Oregon. It feels counterproductive to go back to Mt. Hood but we made these plans months ago and didn't know exactly where we'd be back then. I'm totally fine with it because it's supposed to rain this weekend and I'd rather not hike in that.

Two days later…

DAY 136

We got dropped off at the trail and will begin hiking tomorrow morning. After 3 zeroes, I am raring to go and get this PCT thing over with. It has been an incredible experience but it is getting very cold during the night and staying cold through the day and I am sick of hiking. Though I expect that the eventual end of the trail will be bittersweet, right now I want to finish. The physical discomfort is old. Sore mornings and broken nights of sleep are tiresome and the insides of my ankles are killing me. We basically need to sprint to Canada to finish in time on October 7th. We need to average 21.7 trail miles per day. In the Cascades, that is a full day of hiking and the days are getting much shorter as the winter approaches. Time to dominate these three weeks and finish strong.

DAY 137

Today I started getting very weird back issues just a couple miles into the hike. My lower back is burning intensely. The burn is not painful thankfully but very uncomfortable, it feels like I have a hot water bottle on it or an icy hot patch on it. It starts about 2 miles in every time I begin to hike and only goes away if I sit down for 5 or so minutes and take my backpack off. I mentioned it to Eddie and he said he is feeling the exact same sensation and that it started about a week ago for him. I eventually conclude that this latest ailment is a result of the change in weather, but am confused as to why this didn't happen back at 12,000 feet before Mt. Whitney when it was even colder than it is now. Eddie and I are both experiencing it and sometimes the feeling even extends to my upper back and the tops of my feet. Very weird, but I am just taking many short breaks now instead of a few longer ones. Today we hiked past Mt. Adams and I, perturbed, noticed that the snowline was only about 500 feet higher than where we are hiking. The view of Mt. Adams was breathtaking. The only other time that I've seen Mt. Adams is when Ed and I summitted Mt. Rainier a couple years ago and looked south. When I was hiking alone today I heard the strangest shriek from the valley to my left. I brushed it off but then it repeated a few minutes later. I decided to take a break and keep my video camera on to see if I could capture the sound. I got it on camera and showed it to an old man who was hiking southbound past me. He told me that the sound was an elk lowing. It is elk hunting season right now. Another old man passed me hiking southbound. He told me his name was Sasquatch and that he is a Nobo PCT hiker. He woke up this morning and decided that he's had enough of the trail. He had his Forrest Gump moment "I'm pretty tired. I think I'll go home now." Crazy that he would hike 2200 miles and just decide that he is not going to finish. Onwards, no matter what, to Canada for me.

DAY 138

Today was the most scenic day of my entire life. Though we did more elevation today than we've done in a long while, we were rewarded with a stunning view of Mount Rainier and Mount St. Helens from the Goat Rocks Wilderness. The sunset was the most beautiful thing I've ever seen, a dazzling pink above jagged mountain peaks atop a fluffy bed of cumulus cloud 9 clouds. We were so fortunate to be above the cloud line at that exact spot at that exact time that I feel bad for every other hiker that has hiked the trail before and after me. They didn't experience what we experienced and we are so very blessed and fortunate. The "knife's edge" was some of the sketchier hiking we've done yet. Finally trekked through some snow, our first since the Sierra.

DAY 139

Today we began the descent into the small town of Packwood. We camped above the clouds and woke up to a beautiful sunrise and a clear view of Mt. Rainier in the distance. We hiked down into the clouds and were forced to take an alternate route to Packwood because the PCT is closed for this section due to a fire earlier in the year. I did not mind because the alternate led us past Packwood Lake, an incredible lake with a picturesque island right in the center, similar though smaller than Lake Bled in Slovenia. We called a trail angel named Mama G and she arranged a ride from a guy named Andre who picked us up and drove us to Packwood. I got an enormous hoagie sandwich with steak fries, took a shower, and fell asleep in a cheap motel room.

DAY 140

We woke up in Packwood and got chicken fried steaks at the restaurant. Eddie rated it as a 7.6 out of 10, really good. The hotel guy arranged a ride back to trail at 11 AM. We've set a goal to be 52 miles up the trail by tomorrow so we can make it to Mike Urich Ski Cabin for the night. Our trail friend, Benjamin Button, has a birthday tomorrow and he wants to celebrate at the cabin. To make it 52 miles will be a stretch. We hiked 22 today with an hour or so of night hiking to make tomorrow only a 30 mile day. It is supposed to rain all day tomorrow. I finished *War and Peace* today. What a monster of a book, I very much enjoyed it.

DAY 141

30 mile day with views of Mount Rainier all day. We hiked above the Crystal ski resort where Jenny and I have skied multiple times. Jenny's dad knows the resort by heart and has given me several ski lessons there. It didn't rain at all

today! Those meteorologists have no idea what they're doing. We made it to the cabin but Benjamin Button didn't make it. We met Flat Earth, Arms, Double D, and Gourmet there. The cabin itself was pretty cool but was a total bust in terms of fun. When we got there we were totally exhausted and there wasn't any electricity. I had a horrible night's sleep because there were mice running around all night. I slept on a wooden bench and got maybe 1-2 hours of sleep due to the scurrying of the mice and my paranoia that they would run onto my head.

DAY 142

I woke up to find that a mouse had chewed through one of my backpack hip pockets and nibbled into one of my granola bars. Today really sucked. All the rain that was forecast for yesterday showed up in full force today. The only bright spot was that there was trail magic in the form of a family taking senior pictures for their son up in the mountains. They made us hoagie sandwiches and gave us Doritos. This is the first day that I've had to set up camp in the rain. After slipping and sliding down a hill, everything in my possession was soaked. I'm glad tomorrow night we will be at Snoqualmie Pass and I can dry my stuff out.

DAY 143

Today's hike was brutal because it was another "day before town" hike where my cravings pop up and the day goes by at a snail's pace. My back is still heating up terribly and I'm not certain why. It is bearable though if I take short breaks every few miles to cool down. The only thing that made today better was making it to Snoqualmie Pass and seeing places I actually have been before. We hiked right past the 90 freeway which is the one I take to get to Spokane from Seattle and we hiked through Summit Ski Resort that Eddie says he has skied about 100 times before. I crossed a stream but one of the rocks I stepped on was not stable and I tumbled in the stream and got my legs wet. It was forgotten by the time I crested the hill that overlooks the 90 and the ski resort, what a view and what a feeling! My college buddy Jon met us at the Dru Bru Brewery to drive Marshall and I back to Seattle where we are going to spend the night. I wanted to sleep in my own bed and visit my favorite food haunts but Eddie didn't want to go to Seattle until the trail is finished. I don't really understand, but he is his own man and can do what he wants. We went to XXX burgers and I got the biggest one they had and an extra large orange creamsicle milkshake in a frosted stein.

DAY 144

We did our chores and I shed some weight from my pack by getting rid of my filter plunger, my bug net, my nail clippers, and a few other things that I won't need for the last two weeks of the trail. WE ARE IN THE HOME STRETCH. Stevens pass in 70 miles, Stehekin in 100 after that, then CANADA in 100 more!! We got to Snoqualmie after another ride in Jon's car and immediately started the 70 mile stretch to Stevens Pass. Eddie's mom, Margo, joined us for the first 3 miles and then turned around. We were treated to a nice sunset with views of Rainier, though the trail was pretty gnarly, talus rocks and lots of uphill to contend with. We ended up nighthiking for about an hour to hit our goal for the day.

DAY 145

Today Marshall said the elevation profile didn't look so bad in the morning. I took a look at it and disagreed because there was a big six mile hill. He said "yeah but there's only one hill." Anyways, Eddie and I crushed the hill, but didn't see Marshall for the rest of the day. Apparently he didn't crush the hill very fast and had to set up camp before our goal. It's getting cold and dark earlier and earlier as the winter approaches and we rise in latitude. We've actually been enjoying clear sunny days recently and we are hearing rumors of a dry fall being forecast!

DAY 146

I didn't sleep very well last night and I immediately felt a lack of energy while I tackled the first hill of the day. These Cascades are brutal, long hills followed by long downhills all day climbing up mountains and into valleys. My energy level kept dropping and dropping and my appetite was not cooperating with me. The retching fits started, and soon I could barely walk 2 miles in a row without stopping to take a break. 1 mile on the hills. I knew there was something seriously wrong with me, and I needed to get to civilization fast. We had to complete 22 miles to get down to highway 2 and do it before it got dark at 6:30 PM so we could attempt to get a hitch. It was 4:30 PM and I had 6 miles to go, meaning that I needed to go nonstop for 2 hours straight in order to get down this side trail to highway 2 where Eddie was so we could try and get a hitch. My gas tank was on E but I was motivated to get down to the highway so Ed wouldn't have to give up a hitch on my account. So I began my 6 mile death march down the face of this mountain and I think it was the hardest thing I've had to do yet on this trail. My lack of energy made every step a challenge and I was having trouble with every joint in my body. I eventually made it around 6:45 PM and we miraculously got picked up by an ex-thruhiker who took pity on us and took us to Skykomish. We went to a bar for dinner but I could barely eat my food and left early and flopped onto my motel bed without taking a shower. Thank God I didn't have to set up camp tonight.

DAY 147

Definitely something wrong with me. I have nausea, hourly diarrhea, a lack of appetite, and a lack of energy. This is a terrible time to get sick because we can't afford to slacken our pace right now. Even so, I needed a zero or else I wouldn't be able to function on trail. I spent the day resting in bed and felt better as the day wore on. I am hoping this was only a 24 hour bug. My hourly diarrhea stopped at 8 PM.

DAY 148

I feel much better today, shuttling back to the trail at 8 AM. We got to Stevens Pass and stopped at the lodge for a bit. I've been skiing here with Jenny a few times before. We saw Marshall and he told us he was going to skip up to Stehekin because his feet were shredded from his new shoes. I hiked hoping that my stomach issues were behind me and I was pleasantly surprised that I was feeling pretty decent as I started tackling the day's 18 miles. I suspect my sickness was something called norovirus because the symptoms and the short duration of the sickness both match what happened to me, but there is no way to be sure. We got to the top of Grizzly Peak and took a break. One of the main differences between the AT and the PCT is that the PCT tends to wind to mountain passes whereas the AT goes up to the actual peaks. Some people talk down on the PCT because of that but I am completely happy not having to hike all the way up to the peaks. Grizzly peak is the only actual peak that the PCT officially summits though I've also taken side-trails that went up to the peaks of Mt. Whitney and Mt. Baden Powell. We camped at a beautiful alpine lake and made a campfire and sang songs with some other talented musicians named Meech and Hooch. Classic campfire stuff that doesn't happen as much as I thought it would when I started the trail. A lot of nights there's not enough time, people are too tired, there's a burn ban, the wood is too wet to burn, or people just don't feel like it.

DAY 149

Today was a nice day, not too sunny or too cloudy. But we are hearing rumors that it is going to snow the next two days. I can kind of feel it in the air and the tops of the climbs are very windy and cold. Today my sleeping bag stuff sack started to finally come apart. It's been slowly disintegrating for the last 5 months and it's finally just about unusable. Things are starting to break left and right, holes forming in my pants pockets, one of the ports in my external battery has gone kaput, the socks that I bought at the beginning of the trail are now too full of rips and holes to use, my new shoe got sliced open by a rock at the toe a couple days ago, just everything is falling apart. Good thing there's only a week to go and duct tape lasts about a week. We went 24 miles and camped with Big Bro, the guy from Augsburg.

DAY 150

What a day. Top 5 hardest day on trail with Mt. Whitney, my 42 mile day into Cascade Locks, and my death march into Skykomish also in the top 5. The day started off well enough, then the rain started and the hills started soon after. We did more elevation gain today (5,170 feet) than any other day of the trail, the previous high was about 4,300 feet. Complicating the length of the hills was the muddy condition of the trail. I slipped and fell hard 5 separate times today. One of the falls was particularly bad and I came close to falling off the trail, my whole right leg was hanging off. If I had fell there would luckily have been a switchback about 20 feet down the hill that I would have tumbled onto. Since there was a threat of snow we thought it would be prudent to make it to low elevation tonight so as not to deal with early morning snow and ice the next day. The problem was that we had timed our ascent of the last hill wrong. By the time we summited the 6 mile hill, it was 6:30 PM and already fast losing daylight. The next suitable campsite that was not at the top of the mountain was 4 miles down the other side. So it was a night hike in the pouring rain on a trail that was rough and riddled with fallen trees. One tree that lay across the trail was enormous and must've been about 6 feet in diameter. There was no way around it and it was too big to climb over so the only way to go by was to crawl underneath it in a big mud puddle (the tree was laying at an angle over the trail with 2-3 feet that I could crawl under at the uphill side). The last 3 miles of the day were a night hike. Also, a one-in-a-million woodchip flew right into my eye, irritated my eye for half the day, but it eventually got better.

DAY 151

Today we took a fire detour to Holden Village. 27 more miles with a big 7 mile hill in the middle of the day. They have a communal dinner served from 5-6:30 PM at Holden so I raced the last 14 miles of the day to get there in time for dinner. Didn't take one break for that stretch. The detour itself was beautiful. I got great pictures of a couple glacial lakes. The weather today was decent but I still wore my big blue poncho for most of the day because of the scattered showers. I find it curious that I haven't seen a single deer or large animal in Washington at all. I've heard elk bugles but haven't seen a single deer. After seeing 50-60 in California and Oregon, I am surprised. I ended up getting into Holden around 6:30 PM and happily catching dinner. Holden Village is a retreat center for adults so it has a religious summer camp vibe to it. They ripped us off by charging $100 each for a room, but I was so wet and tired that I paid it anyways. Eddie didn't get in til 7:30 PM.

DAY 152

We had a pancake breakfast at Holden and took the 10:30 bus to Lucerne and then caught the Lake Chelan ferry to the awesome little town of Stehekin (the fire detour took us off the PCT). Stehekin has a store, a restaurant, an excellent bakery, and that's about it. It is only accessible via ferry and floatplane so it is unique. The motel was sold out so we camped about a 10 minute walk from the town in the permitted campground. Here we finally had WiFI after 4 days of no communication, but the WiFi quickly broke down. We resupplied and took a quick nap when a sudden squall rolled into the town, high winds and driving rain. Good thing I was in my tent. We had an excellent celebratory dinner (last trail town!) with Big Bro and Flat Earth and a couple bottles of wine. I Facetimed Jenny but didn't realize my phone battery was low. It died and when I walked back to my campsite, I realized that my phone is also my flashlight and it was a completely pitch dark walk. I stumbled around for a couple minutes when I luckily came upon an English couple named Stuff Sack and Apollo who had a light but couldn't remember where the campsite was. Perfect! We easily found it 10 minutes later. That was a first for me, being without a flashlight in the pitch darkness and needing to walk somewhere. Just 4 days and 91 miles left.

DAY 153

We had breakfast, frantically used the Wifi when it started working again to communicate with Jenny and Marshall, and caught the 9:30 bus back to the trail, stopping first for an excellent cinnamon roll at the bakery. We have a good group of hikers heading back to trail and we are all planning on reaching the terminus on Saturday the 6th. Big Bro, Flat Earth, Double D, Arms, Gourmet, Stuff Sack, Apollo, Balloons, Snow White, me, Ed, and Marshall. Marshall met us at the end of today where we hit some trail magic provided by a guy named Mad Baker and Eddie's cousin named Alex. Chili, hot chocolate, and Doritos, and hanging out in Alex's car with the heater on. We saw a little snow on the trail at the end of the day and are seeing it just above us on the mountains, we'll be hiking into it tomorrow and it is getting damn cold.

DAY 154

We hiked up past the snowline early in the day, the day is blue skies but below freezing, so it is hard to take long breaks. The scenery is incredible, snowcapped mountains in panorama. We climbed the last big hills of the trail today, the ones after today are dinky 2 mile ones. The end is very near and it is very very cold. My pen is not working very well because of the cold I think.

DAY 155

Last night was absolutely freezing, I could barely sleep and I was hearing weird animal noises outside the tent, probably goats. Eddie had a night terror or something because at one point he screamed, but he doesn't remember doing it. Packing up camp was so cold I couldn't feel my toes or fingers afterwards, and it took me a mile or two of hiking to get back to normal temperature. Today we tried to tackle the last fire closure, a 21 mile trek through a frozen forest. It was a bummer because the normal PCT route is amazingly beautiful mountain scenery (and 4 miles shorter) and instead we walked through another forest. Lots of those on this trip. We got within 3 miles of our goal for the day, Woody Pass, and stopped short because the last 3 miles were uphill and Woody Pass looked crazy cold from afar. We camped at the lower elevation and resolved to get up early to try and finish the trail at 12 PM tomorrow and meet the Canadians, Big Bro, Flat Earth, and some other hikers there. We are planning to play *Good Riddance* by Green Day when we get there.

DAY 156

Last. Day. We forced ourselves to wake up early, and were hiking by 7 AM. I was in hiking legend mode so I quickly sped past Marshall and Eddie. There were places where the snow was a foot deep, but the trail is well worn with the footstep outlines of many hikers before me to step in. Today is Saturday and there is supposed to be a big winter storm on Monday, and I wonder if this section will be passable for the hikers after me. I talked to a guy named Rebel from Alabama for a few miles. There were 14 miles to the border from our campsite. I did it in under 4 hours, getting there about 45 minutes before the others. I waited a couple tenths of a mile before the border for Eddie to catch up with me. Canada!!! It was a surreal feeling as we walked up to the completion monument. There were a few hikers there already cheering loudly as Ed and I approached. We took pictures, recorded our trail jam, signed the trail log and left ASAP after that as we were getting cold. We hiked the last 9 miles into Canada to the closest road and were picked up by Jenny and Luke, a long awaited reunion. I am looking forward to many zero days in my near future.

DAY 157
FINAL REFLECTION IN DIARY

People have different motivations to hike the trail. My primary objectives were to read books and lose weight. I listened to 71 audiobooks along the journey and lost a whopping 52 pounds. The feelings of knowledgeableness and healthiness that I have right now are incredible feelings. I have a very high sense of self esteem, and feel like I can tackle any challenge. My cathartic experience happened on day 80 in the Northern Sierra, when I realized the business idea I've been working on for the past couple years would make a better book than a business. My next challenge is to flex some of my dormant creative muscles and write a book good enough to be published. Based on the 50 plus nonfiction books I read, I'm pretty certain that I'll be able to write a quality book. I have so many people to thank for helping me along the journey, chiefly Jenny and my parents. I will send thank you notes to all the trail angels who gave me sweet respite in my time of need. Although the trail has been devastating for my pocketbook, I feel enriched in so many other ways and feel like the trail was a success in every way. Before the trail, I made a pros and cons list:

Pros:
- Gain startup and history knowledge through audiobooks
- Keep a journal
- Lose weight
- Challenge myself and get out of comfort zone
- Good career transition
- Do it without the help of painkillers or coffee
- Time with Ed and Marshall
- Write songs with Ed
- Become a better outdoorsman
- Know how to survive without modern stuff
- Spiritual reflection
- Reduce reliance on your phone
- Help NFL addiction
- See California/Oregon/Washington nature
- Bucket List
- Grow a Big Beard

I can say with certainty that I achieved 14 out of 16 of these pros. I didn't write many songs with Eddie (we just didn't feel like it and we didn't have time) and I don't think I helped my phone reliance issue at all. I used the phone constantly throughout the trip for my audiobooks and guthook navigation app. Everything else was achieved. Even though keeping a diary felt like a chore most of the time, I'm very happy I did it. It is something I will save forever, and read from time to time. My body held up impressively well. I expect my ankles to be a lingering pain for me, but my knees and back are feeling fine right now. Onto the next adventure!

THE END.

www.ingramcontent.com/pod-product-compliance
Lightning Source LLC
Chambersburg PA
CBHW020902080526
44589CB00011B/408